SURVIVING THE CUT

An Executive's Guide to Successful Job Hunting in Today's Tough Market

KEVIN J. MURPHY

BANTAM BOOKS

NEW YORK • TORONTO • LONDON • SYDNEY • AUCKLAND

SURVIVING THE CUT
A Bantam Book/July 1991

Bantam Books are published by Bantam Books, a division of Bantam
Doubleday Dell Publishing Group, Inc. Its trademark, consisting of the
words "Bantam Books" and the portrayal of a rooster, is Registered in
U.S. Patent and Trademark Office and in other countries. Marca Regis-
trada. Bantam Books, 666 Fifth Avenue, New York, New York 10103.

PRINTED IN THE UNITED STATES OF AMERICA

BVG   0 9 8 7 6 5 4 3 2 1

CDK Associates & Consultants, Inc.

KEVIN J. MURPHY
PRESIDENT & CEO

TO: All Highly Qualified Job
Applicants

RE: *Surviving The Cut*

Over the years, I have seen many sincere, hard-working individuals unknowingly lose out on a job opportunity because of inexperience and misconceptions.

As a new entrant into the job market, it is understandable that you might make errors during your search. But today, with the significant number of candidates competing for each job, you need every edge to rise above the crowd.

This book will provide you with practical insights into many subtle actions that can disqualify you as a candidate. When you read *Surviving The Cut*, please take special note of the anecdotes in each chapter. The stories are true, and in each case, the careless actions of the candidates cost them an opportunity to stay in the hunt.

During your search, try to be flexible, and never overlook the little things that can cut you from the competition.

I wish you the best of health and happiness in your pursuits. And, in the near future, may you survive the cut and make the team of your choice.

Sincerely,

Kevin J. Murphy

Kevin J. Murphy

P.O. Box 1523 • 198 Main Street • Salem, NH 03079 • (603) 898-9372

To my wife Dolores, and my children Kevin, Christina, and Kerri for their love and understanding.

Acknowledgments

No project can come to fruition without the help and support of friends and associates. *Surviving The Cut* was conceived, written, and produced in a three-month period, a remarkable accomplishment for a publication of this nature.

Our driving force was to get this publication into the hands of all the unfortunate job seekers who have been victimized by slow economic times, downsizing, and the phasing out of different industries.

Surviving The Cut was coordinated and edited by Ed Strenk. Ed's dedication and long hours were critical to bringing this project in on time. He is not only a good friend but also a wonderful writer and sounding board.

The professionals at Bantam Doubleday Dell, especially Becky Cabaza, Michael Cecilione, and Jim Plumeri, deserve a round of applause for their hard work under heavy deadlines.

I would also like to thank the Bantam Doubleday Dell sales group, particularly John Ziccardi and George Harris, for their support and belief in this project. Selling isn't an easy task in today's world and this dedicated group of people made the difference.

Finally, I would like to thank all my friends, clients, and associates who urged me to pursue the project of bringing these important job seeking concepts to people who need help in securing a job in a competitive market.

Kevin J. Murphy

Contents

Introduction

Barbara was frustrated and confused. After advancing
to the final interviews for several sales positions, she
eventually lost out to the other candidates, many of
whom appeared less qualified. A solid performer for
over ten years, this forty-two-year-old divorced mother
of three had always made her quota selling computer
software products. In fact, on several occasions, she
even received awards from both her company and customers for outstanding performance. Barbara knew her
references were good and she had a wonderful track
record of accomplishments.

Yet something that Barbara could not identify was
turning off potential employers. Fortunately for Barbara, a humane recruiter unfolded the mystery. Checks
on Barbara's credit by the employers revealed several
instances of foreclosures and repossessions that were
being interpreted as acts of indiscretion. What these
employers didn't know was that Barbara's former husband, because of problems with gambling and drugs,

1

had left her with many unpaid debts. Armed now with this new information, Barbara consciously raised the credit issue in her next interview and explained her plight. She not only gained the respect and admiration of her potential employer, she also landed the job.

Barbara's case is not unusual.* With so many qualified candidates available, companies will not have either the inclination or the need to investigate problems that on the surface could have reasonable explanations.

Over the next several years, one out of every three professionals like Barbara earning in excess of $50,000 could be forced to look for a new job in an oversupplied market.

Now the bad news . . . Most of these individuals will be over forty years of age, possess five to twenty years of service with their current employer, and have no comprehension of what it takes to beat their competition in the battle for getting jobs. Even worse, many of the unemployed will be misled by job coaches, outplacement firms, recruiters, and publications that focus entirely on how to search for a job *instead of how to avoid actions that eliminate them from the field.*

Make no mistake about it, with unemployment rates exceeding 9 percent for highly paid positions, *landing a job will be a function of staying in the hunt more than possessing eye-popping qualifications.*

Mergers, acquisitions, and downsizing strategies are creating fierce competition for key positions. Jobs that once required only three years of general experience and an undergraduate degree now have specifications that necessitate a graduate degree and specific experience.

---

* *To protect the privacy of everyone involved, names and other identifying details have been changed in the cases reported on.*

As one of our clients who runs a building-supply company stated in setting the stage for a new search, "We're looking for a well-educated generalist with specific experience in our product markets . . . somebody who can call on major contractors and carry business to our company."

Not only did our client find a salesperson that fit that description, they also paid him 10 percent less than the individual he replaced even though he possessed better qualifications and experience.

But all is not lost. There are, and will continue to be, thousands of wonderful opportunities in the years ahead. The key is to put yourself in a winning position by avoiding the knockout punches that can cost you a job.

In conjunction with my consulting practice, during the past five years alone I have personally reviewed 30,000 résumés, interviewed in excess of 1,500 potentials, and checked references on hundreds of candidates. Our executive searches were conducted for companies in diverse industries, such as health care, plastics, chemicals, automotive, textiles, building products, and telecommunications.

In all these assignments, regardless of the markets, industries, or technologies, the hiring process became one of elimination instead of qualification. The number of players is staggering. *The bottom line—individuals have to develop an approach that will keep them in the running for a job.*

This philosophy is most pronounced during the screening process where employers, because of the significant number of applicants, look for quick fixes to eliminate candidates. For example, a small, two-inch employment ad in a major newspaper like the *Boston Globe* or the *Wall Street Journal* can generate over five hundred responses for a single position.

If you had to initially screen the responses to such an advertisement, would you be inclined to wade through and read each letter and résumé?

Well, one of our client's secretaries didn't think it was necessary and found a solution. In the process of filling a key telecommunications product–management position, she discarded over 70 percent of the respondents based on the condition of the envelopes, the grammar in the cover letters, and the print quality of the résumés. Her feeling was that "if the first contact is not good, what can we expect after they come on board?" Notice? Nothing was mentioned about qualifications. In fact, this secretary to the vice-president of sales had absolutely no comprehension of the qualifications and education requirements of this high-paying position. *But she made the call and decided who would get cut and eliminated from the competition.*

Surviving The Cut describes in detail the most common mistakes that can hurt your chances of securing that important job in a competitive global market. Many elements of an employment search may seem minor to you, but in the competitive world of the job hunt, those details can mean the difference between making the team or getting cut.

The objective, then, is to increase your awareness of all the subtleties that can help you survive the initial cut, shine in the tryouts, and make the team.

Surviving The Cut is divided into three parts. The first part, "Surviving the Initial Cut," deals specifically with the search and screening process. This section covers every aspect of soliciting employment from addressing the envelope to securing the interview. You will learn how to stay in the running and secure an invitation to the tryout.

Part two, "How to Shine During the Tryout," walks you through the interview process and highlights the proper etiquette once you're on the employer's playing field. In this section you will read about Harry, the leading candidate for a $150,000 position as VP of marketing for a major automotive-parts supplier. He didn't make the cut because he complained to the president's assistant about how long it took her to get him a cup of coffee. "The executive suite will have its own machine once I come on board" was Harry's solution to the problem. Too bad he never got a chance to implement his suggestion. This part will also heighten your awareness of silent interviewers like the president's assistant, the receptionist, and even the cafeteria cashier who may be asked for input even though they are not part of the formal hiring process.

The third part, "Making the Team," covers all of the steps after the personal interview from writing a follow-up letter to selecting references. Contrary to popular belief, reference checks are not a rubber-stamp procedure. In fact, reference checks eliminate 10 to 20 percent of all prospective candidates, even when supplied by the candidate. This figure may seem high, but you'll never get a true feeling for this statistic because companies rarely expose poor references for fear of legal retaliation. The harsh reality is, at turn-down time, you may hear: "Your qualifications are great, but we decided to promote from within," or "We changed the job description," or "We eliminated the position through reorganization." In actuality, the position may still exist, but one of your actions alienated someone during the interview process.

To be an all-star, you have to get invited to the tryout, survive the cut, and then make the team. By following the steps outlined in this book, you will be coached to avoid those actions that can give your competition the edge. Potential employers will never realize the depths of your talent unless you're given an opportunity to play. Now get ready to dig in and condition yourself to win.

PART I

Surviving
the Initial Cut

CHAPTER 1

A Quick Start and Realistic Expectations Are Critical to a Successful Job Search

On your mark . . . Get set . . . Go.

Like a sprinter, you need to be off like a shot the moment you find out your services are no longer needed. Any delay in starting your job search could result in lost opportunities. Time is of the essence when you're out of work.

But mistakenly, too many executives take time off before they commence an active search, sometimes to go sailing for the summer or skiing for the winter. Some people need to sit back and reflect. Others negotiate lucrative severance packages and have the confidence they can find a job at will. Then there are the ones who are just confused and apprehensive because looking for a job is a new and frightening experience.

———————— ❖ ————————

MISCONCEPTION

*Potential employers will admire you for taking time off
between jobs.*

REALITY

*Taking time off between jobs indicates you lack a sense of
urgency, focus, and aggressiveness.*

———————— ❖ ————————

Whatever the reason, you need to be keenly aware that taking time off not only removes you from the market, it also raises concerns for potential employers.

Putting off the search sends a signal that you lack a sense of urgency in one of the most important aspects of your life. The employer then has to wonder if you would react the same way when a critical part has to go out the next day to avoid shutting down a customer's plant.

False and delayed starts also raise questions about your commitment, focus, and aggressiveness. Employers love to hire people who demonstrate their desire to work. The greater the gap on your résumé between your last day of work and the time you apply for a position, the more likely you will have to answer in-depth questions concerning your activities during the period of unemployment. And by the way, bragging about a huge severance package does little to justify taking time off, particularly during the summer months.

If you are shy about getting your search on the road, seek the help of professional recruiters, self-help groups, or friends and associates who have been through similar experiences. Remember, you are not alone in your quest to find a job, so make every effort to keep your spirits high and your attitude positive. Be aggressive and don't just sit back and expect things to happen. Severance pay runs out faster than you think, and the more time you spend jobless, the more your confidence will wane. In addition, potential employers will begin to wonder why others haven't picked up on your talents.

———————— ❖ ————————

MISCONCEPTION

Good jobs are easy to find if you have great qualifications.

REALITY

The job market is crowded with candidates who also possess great qualifications.

———————— ❖ ————————

Now . . . For all you top dogs who have earned six figures for many years, get ready for a slice of reality. You are now on the other side of the desk. The companies you are soliciting have functioned in the past without your help and knowledge.

Don't forget . . . *You are the one trying to make the team.*

In a tough market, the key words are *flexible* and *realistic.* You must be flexible and willing to consider positions that are lower in stature and may require sacrifices, such as relocating or even forfeiting a fancy title. More important, you must be realistic with your compensation and expectations for your new job. Setting your sights too high will limit your objectivity. You may even pass up a good opportunity because you think something better might be on the horizon.

A case in point: Jonathan, a forty-five-year-old marketing executive, was a key player in a $500M company that was purchased by a $5 billion conglomerate. The consolidation of the companies resulted in the elimination of his position as VP of product planning. For the first time in twenty-one years, this father of three college students was faced with the task of finding a job.

Shortly after he was laid off, a $75M telecommunications client I represented interviewed Jonathan for a top marketing position. Throughout the meeting, it was clear to both me and the hiring company that Jonathan felt the position of VP of marketing in this smaller company was beneath him. Eventually, he turned down a generous offer from this company. The compensation package was only 15 percent less than his former salary. My client proceeded to fill the position with an

———— ❖ ————

MISCONCEPTION

Employers will think you are a soft touch if you accept a lower salary.

REALITY

Employers will respect you if your expectations are realistic, demonstrating a desire to work.

———— ❖ ————

equally qualified person at a significantly lower salary. Jonathan continued on his quest for the perfect job.

Six months later, almost to the day, I received a distressed call from Jonathan inquiring if the marketing position was still available. After hearing the bad news, Jonathan asked if I knew of any other opportunities in his field. Jonathan admitted, "I shouldn't have passed up the opportunity at the telecommunications company," but he had been reluctant to accept a low offer so early in his search. Several months later, Jonathan landed an assignment as a product manager but for 30 percent less than the first offer he received almost a year earlier.

Jonathan fell prey to the most deadly mistake that high fliers make after losing touch with the job market for many years. He misjudged the value of his talents and misread the market.

Industries are constantly changing and technology alters the needs for specific expertise. Nuclear engineering was one of the most sought-after disciplines in the late seventies. Software professionals were in strong demand throughout the eighties. Environmental engineering may be a growing field in the years ahead. Times change.

Whatever the case, make sure you sit down and set your job search strategy by becoming fully cognizant of the changing market conditions in your target industries.

Regardless of how extensive your education, or how deep your talents and experience, be realistic and recognize that every potential employer doesn't have the need or financial resources to pay for each and every one of your skills. Realistic expectations will keep you on the road to that new job provided you don't get detoured by your ego and pride.

Don't be insulted by the first offer you get. Remember, your negotiating base for future jobs is significantly strengthened if you are gainfully employed. That first offer may be the only one you receive.

CHAPTER 2

Using the Right Tools
for the "Write" Job

Certainly, the content of a résumé and a cover letter is crucial, but remember that secretary who eliminated 70 percent of her company's potential employees based on the *appearance* of the envelopes and stationery that carried their credentials—it happens.

The best laid plans in the world can crumble if you don't use the appropriate tools from start to finish. How often have you had to fix a household appliance or toy only to find out your traditional screwdriver doesn't work well on Phillips head screws?

Remember that when you are trying to do a credible job of attracting the attention of potential employers, you must use the proper writing and copying tools to address an envelope, compose the cover letter, and present your résumé.

———— ❖ ————

MISCONCEPTION

Your eye-popping qualifications will get an employer's attention regardless of the vehicle you use to present them.

REALITY

Regardless of your qualifications, correspondence that is difficult to read will not get action.

———— ❖ ————

So, when you're ready to prepare and start your presentation, a few items may need to be discarded from your workbench in favor of more reliable, state-of-the-art tools.

The Truth About Dot Matrix Printers and Circa 1975 PCs

If your children are still using your computer and printer to design dot matrix posters for their bedrooms, it's time to move on.

Résumés and cover letters produced on ancient printers look old and outdated. In addition, the print quality, darkness, and condition of perforated paper make a poor impression on the people who initially screen your letters and résumés. During the time it took to write this chapter, we received ten such résumés that were illegible because of the light print that obviously came off one of the dinosaur dot matrix printers. Letters produced on these printers reproduce poorly and blur when faxed.

Many word-processor typewriters, such as the models made by Brother, Smith Corona, and Panasonic, produce a professional-quality type style. This gives the impression that each letter is individualized. These products also have storage capabilities that allow you to develop a variety of personalized cover letters. This appropriate tool can give you that professional image for a minimal cost of under $500.

Finally, there is nothing wrong with using a typewriter provided the quality and definition of the print is professional. But remember, call on the services of a friend or spouse to proofread. Most of us have become heavily dependent on the use of automatic spelling checkers.

———— ❖ ————

MISCONCEPTION

*Colored stationery provides you with an excellent
differentiating factor that will grab the attention of the
readers.*

REALITY

*Over 40 percent of the job-hunting population uses colored
stationery. So much for differentiation.*

———— ❖ ————

Colored Envelopes and Stationery Don't Differentiate

The problem here is that too many people have read books or listened to professionals who preach differentiation as the key to getting noticed in a job hunt.

One of the first ways inexperienced job seekers try to stand out from the pack is by using colored paper in the packaging of their qualifications. A quick survey of our files would reveal that over 40 percent of the job-seeking population uses colored stationery and envelopes. So much for differentiation!

The major problems posed by colored stationery are readability and reproducibility. Blues and grays, and some shades of ivory, create a screened background when copied or faxed. Imagine a personnel manager who has an ocean of résumés and letters to swim through. If yours is murky, forget it. Faxes and copiers don't do justice to colored paper.

Besides colors, heavily textured finishes, linens, and stamped stock above the 24-pound weight are difficult to fold, which results in wide creases that look terrible when unfolded. Also, stay away from erasable paper that looks and feels like onionskin. Save that for your children's book reports.

The safest bet with which to present your wares is a quality, bright white bond or lightly textured stock. Remember, there is a difference between cost and price, and the price you'll pay for cutting costs in your presentation materials could be significant.

Commercial Reproduction Machines
Need to Be in Good Condition

Most candidates do not have access to state-of-the-art copiers and have to resort to the public machines found in drugstores, office-supply outlets, and libraries. Nothing's wrong with this provided the machines are maintained to deliver quality copies.

Also, there are many small printers in most towns that can provide assistance in selecting stationery and printing. If you shop around, you will find a printer that caters to the needs of the job seeker. These printers also have state-of-the-art copiers and fax machines that can be utilized if an employer or agency requests an instant copy of your credentials.

Forwarding résumés that look too much like copies can send a signal that your search is the shotgun approach of mailing hundreds of cheaply reproduced résumés to anyone with an opening. Seek out a reliable copy machine that will make all of your correspondence look original.

Using letter-quality printers with neutral stationery is the best tool to minimize your chances of being knocked from the competition. Your first correspondence must project a progressive, professional image.

Take inventory of your tools and use the ones that make every piece of correspondence look custom-made and professional.

CHAPTER 3

The Envelope . . . Please

You may never get a second chance to make a good first impression.

A simple envelope can set the stage for an employer's first and possible last impression of you as a job candidate. The all-important envelope is the first piece of evidence a potential employer has to gauge your appearance, clarity, attention to detail, and character in approaching an important assignment like finding yourself work.

I used to think individuals applying for a $50,000 to $200,000 position would make certain that the envelopes containing their résumés and letters would be perfect. Was I wrong!

---------------- ❖ ----------------

MISCONCEPTION

Handwritten envelopes are a nice personal touch.

REALITY

Handwritten envelopes present a poor first image and often result in errors and misspellings.

---------------- ❖ ----------------

A few years ago, because of a heavy workload and 1,500 résumés sitting on my desk, I began looking at the envelope as a disqualification factor in an effort to save time in the screening process. For two months, we compared candidates to their envelope presentation and a very interesting correlation surfaced. The envelopes turned out to be a direct reflection of their attitude toward such things as neatness, accuracy, and urgency.

Individuals who submitted shabby envelopes actually appeared disorganized in person. Also, people who addressed envelopes with incorrect information and errors had difficulty communicating their specific accomplishments and qualifications.

We continue to test our observations with consistent results. Therefore, more than ever before, we believe in using the envelope as a major tool for initially screening candidates for key positions. In addition to our company, over twenty of our clients now use envelope guidelines to eliminate people for management or sales positions paying over $50,000.

So before you sit down to address your next envelope, consider the following practices that can hinder your chances of landing a high-paying job.

Handwriting envelopes.
A person seeking a $50,000 position should have both the professional attitude and resources to use a typewriter or a word processor to address a neat envelope. Having your children or spouse handwriting envelopes in an effort to save time while responding to multiple job opportunities will not make the grade. Also, poor handwriting can be difficult to read and can result in misinterpretations and errors.

———— ❖ ————

MISCONCEPTION

Big, oversized envelopes are a wonderful way to differentiate yourself.

REALITY

Big envelopes are hard to handle both at the post office and inside the employer's business. They also don't fit in mailboxes, requiring and extra effort to retrieve them.

———— ❖ ————

It's simple. Handwritten envelopes don't get a response because they show a lack of initiative and professionalism.

Ignoring errors and misspellings.

A great philosopher once stated, "When all else is lost, the one thing they can't take away is your name." That's true until someone misspells it on an envelope. Butchering a name or a job title can be perceived as a lack of respect for the individual and his or her position. Many people who have worked long and hard to achieve the status of vice-president get very sensitive when they are referred to as a manager.

It is a fair assumption that such flagrant errors will only foreshadow your lack of urgency and attention to detail.

Envelopes that have misspellings or incorrect information seldom get a second look.

Using your present company's envelope/stationery.

Oh, no! You're a thief. Yes! Using your present company's envelope will be interpreted as a lack of honesty and discretion. The prospective employer might think, "What else did he or she steal from the company" or "What will he or she steal from us?"

You may think there is good reason for using your company's paper, such as the stationery is obsolete because of a change in logo or each employee is given a quantity for personal use. Unfortunately, you may never get a chance to explain this fact.

———— ❖ ————

MISCONCEPTION

Using your former employer's stationery and postage meter shows you had a good relationship.

REALITY

Using a former employer's stationery and postage meter can be interpreted as an act of indiscretion or outright support to get you out of the company.

———— ❖ ————

Stamping the envelope with your current employer's stamp machine.

This common practice is an issue that also focuses on your discretion because it raises the question, "Is this person financing a job search with his or her present employer's resources?"

Our experience shows that 90 percent of the correspondence we receive on machine-stamped company envelopes and stationery is from people sponsored by outplacement programs. Surely being part of an outplacement program is not necessarily negative, but it will certainly intensify the investigation process to determine why you're not one of the survivors at your present company.

Using stamps or stickers that make an emotional or political statement.

Even a well-respected charity like the United Way has its detractors. A stamp with a United Way slogan could alienate a decision maker whose family or friends may have a negative attitude toward this group. Those return-address stickers or stamps that have an organization's logo or slogan should be saved for holidays, birthdays, or personal mail.

The final knock-down punch can be delivered by those *big manila envelopes* that don't fit easily into mailboxes. They are hard to open and usually contain a mountain of information that may seem frightening to climb. Plus, did you ever notice how the big envelopes tear and shred the other materials in the mailbox?

Some experts tell candidates to differentiate them-selves with big envelopes, but when you aggravate a secretary or a mailroom clerk with the cumbersome envelope, that nonstandard envelope may be your one-way ticket to the wastebasket.

You should also be aware that envelopes can re-main part of a permanent file. Therefore, they must look professional and clean. Envelopes are often used to tally the number of responses from ads that appear in different newspapers or journals. They can also pro-vide documentation if your potential employer is con-tacted by an overzealous recruiter who tries to claim a placement fee after you've made direct contact.

Remember, that envelope is your personal vehicle for carrying important correspondence to your poten-tial employer. A clean, neatly typed business envelope with a common postal stamp will be your first positive step in gaining an invitation to the tryout.

CHAPTER 4

The Cover Letter . . .
Your First Chance to Make a
Lasting Impression

Whether you're reacting to an employment ad, an introduction from a networking partner, or a request for a résumé by an employment agency, all job inquiries must be accompanied by a well-orchestrated cover letter.

Other than your envelope, a cover letter is the first piece of evidence a potential employer can use to gauge your professionalism and ability to communicate with the written word. Unfortunately, what most inexperienced job seekers don't understand is that incorrect assumptions, errors, and the extensive use of the first person (I, me, or my) can have a greater impact on your potential employer's perception of you than the actual contents of the letter.

———— ❖ ————

MISCONCEPTION

Addressing people by their first names in the salutation will show you are an informal, friendly person who immediately gets down to business.

REALITY

First names should be reserved for your close friends and associates. Informality could be misinterpreted as disrespect.

———— ❖ ————

Therefore, it is critical to avoid many of the knock-down blows that can transmit the wrong signals and paint an incorrect picture of your personality.

Realize that it is *not what you say, but how you write it* that determines if you will receive further consideration.

After conducting extensive research with human resource professionals, we have compiled a list of the seven most deadly sins that candidates unknowingly commit when they compose the all-important cover letter:

1. Familiar or friendly greetings
2. Gender miscues
3. Insincere and glowing comments
4. Lengthy letters
5. Unsolicited personal references
6. Extensive use of the first person
7. Grammatical errors and misspellings

Familiar or Friendly Greetings

Familiarity breeds contempt. Yes, addressing individuals by their first names is making an assumption that formality is unimportant to them.

Letters and salutations should remain formal until such time as the recipients tell you otherwise. An executive who insists on being addressed as "Mr." by his top-performing subordinates will not take kindly to an outsider writing "Dear Marvin." You can't go wrong with Mr. or Ms. even when the first name of the person is given in an employment ad.

———— ❖ ————

MISCONCEPTION

A cover letter is not as important as your résumé.

REALITY

*Your résumé will never get read if the cover letter
is poorly presented.*

———— ❖ ————

Gender Miscues

On the surface, this blunder might not seem like a big deal. However, mistaking gender can be an indication that you are careless and have a tendency to react before you have all the facts.

Many common names like Chris and Terry can be male or female. Addressing a woman as Mr., or a man as Ms., can hurt a relationship before it has time to develop. This problem is also compounded when people use initials instead of names. For example, an ad might read:

Please reply to M. L. Smith, Director of Personnel

When in doubt, call the company and clarify the gender of the person. If you can't track down the company or the individual, it is appropriate to write: Dear M. L. Smith.

Insincere and Glowing Comments

Sending a letter that patronizes the recipient shines through as being insincere. Making statements like "Your company is great" or "You have a reputation that is second to none" won't help your cause, especially if the company is going through hard times or experiencing a heavy turnover of personnel. You have no concrete basis to comment accurately on a company until you meet the people and evaluate the working environment. Save the accolades for the follow-up letter after you've had a chance to meet the potential employer and evaluate the situation.

—————— ❖ ——————

MISCONCEPTION

The more details you can cram into a cover letter, the better your chances that something will pique the reader's interest.

REALITY

The longer your cover letter, the less likely it will be read completely.

—————— ❖ ——————

Lengthy Letters

The hypothesis here: Shorter is better. Concise letters are more likely to be read. Long, flowing dissertations rarely receive cover-to-cover attention. Brief letters should be the benchmark if you are applying for an executive or sales position.

Let's face it, top executives are paid to make decisions, not to write reports describing the decisions. Salespeople are compensated to bring in orders, not to write "How to" chapters on sales strategies.

For a top position, a cover letter that is any longer than three paragraphs is too lengthy. Your statements should be concise, professional, and polite. Stick to the basics. State your interest, provide a little background that will tease the reader, and end with a request for a meeting.

Another important aspect of short cover letters is using key industry words. These words could relate to state-of-the-art technology, such as SONET in telecommunications or TQM in manufacturing. But weighing down your letters with jargon and acronyms is a big mistake. Write so that the reader won't have to stop and say, "What the hell is he talking about?"

Another good approach when you are applying for a sales or management position is to include the names of recognizable customers. For example, if you are competing for a top sales position in a company that is a major supplier to the automotive industry, make certain names like GM and Ford appear in the cover letter. Because of significant supplier consolidations, insight into a customer's operation is a big selling point that will attract the immediate attention of potential employers.

———————— ❖ ————————

MISCONCEPTION

It is a good idea to include letters of recommendation with your initial correspondence.

REALITY

Letters of recommendation mean little to seasoned recruiters and can in fact detract from your perception as a viable candidate.

———————— ❖ ————————

Unsolicited Personal References

This is one of the quickest ways to eliminate yourself from the race. Sending copies of reference letters is presumptuous and indicates a total naïveté on your part regarding the perception of these letters by potential employers.

Any astute recruiter knows full well that 99 percent of all recommendations are written at the request of the discharged employee. Worse yet, over 50 percent of the letters are composed by the job seeker and not the former employer. How many times have you heard a boss tell an employee who was being let go, "Just write up what you want me to say and I'll sign it"?

Letters of recommendation are not only useless, they also send a covert signal that you had problems in the past and wanted to clear your name in writing.

Avoid sending letters of recommendation. If potential employers find you to be a viable candidate, they will request references soon enough.

Extensive Use of the First Person

In an effort to remove the monotony of reading hundreds of cover letters and résumés, our company keeps track of certain applicant accomplishments. We call it our "Candidate Olympics". Here are a few appropriate categories for our discussion.

Category	Olympic Record
Most colleges attended without ever earning a degree	6
Most employers in a ten-year period	7
Longest résumé (# of pages)	9
Greatest use of "I" and "my" in a one-page cover letter	23

———— ❖ ————

MISCONCEPTION

Frequent use of the first person (I, me or my) in the cover letter will show you really have confidence in yourself.

REALITY

Extensive use of the first person turns off the reader and can send the signal that you might not be a team player.

———— ❖ ————

That's right. One individual used the first person twenty-three times in a twenty-five-line cover letter.

I am enclosing my résumé and I am interested in the position advertised . . . I attribute my success to my leadership abilities . . . I am prepared to demonstrate my talent and I would like to discuss my experiences and my strengths . . . Please contact me at my home so I can meet with you to explain my interests in your company.

What jumps off the page are all the "I's" that not only demonstrate subjectivity but also truly distract the reader. In addition, relying on the first person locks you into using opinionated phrases, such as "I think," "I feel," and "In my opinion." There is nothing wrong with having opinions unless they are incorrect, inappropriate, or offensive to the reader.

However, you can use the first person when you are describing a specific fact or accomplishment.

- My sales exceeded quota for five years running.
- I was awarded "Manager of the Year" for reducing manufacturing rejects by 50 percent.

Another problem with overloading a letter with the "I" syndrome is creating the perception that you're a lone ranger. Statements like "Through my efforts alone, our company grew by 25 percent in a difficult economic climate" can send up a flare revealing that you may not be a team player. Stress the corporate "we" and "our" in your letters. "Through the efforts of our group, we were able to expand our sales by 25 percent in a tough market."

Because of cutbacks in staffs and reduction in overhead, companies are looking for loyal, team players who can wear a number of different hats.

Grammatical Errors and Misspellings

Finally, make sure your letter is free of careless grammatical errors and misspellings. Technical errors in your cover letter demonstrate a lack of attention to detail while raising serious questions about your level of professionalism.

Cover letters are meant to attract attention and pique an employer's interest, not to close the sale. A concise, objective, and professional letter will draw attention to your qualifications instead of highlighting your shortcomings.

One final point: Always ask another person to review and assess your letters objectively. You may be surprised to find out that what you are trying to say is not the same as what the reader is reading.

CHAPTER 5

The Résumé—A Balance Sheet of Your Credentials

A wise old friend once told me, "Too much of anything is bad for you." Too much money fosters greed, too much work can lead to burnout, and too much rich food can cause heart disease.

You won't find a more appropriate philosophy once you begin to develop your résumé. Like the famous line from *Dragnet*, "Just the facts," a résumé should provide a snapshot of your background and education, not a detailed description telling how you reached your accomplishments.

The only objective of a résumé should be to attract the attention of a potential employer and secure a personal interview.

---- ❖ ----

MISCONCEPTION

A résumé should be a complete summary of all your qualifications and employers during the past thirty years.

REALITY

Only highlights of your most recent employment history have real value to potential employers.

---- ❖ ----

With this in mind, our next step will not be a dissertation focusing on the correct way to construct a résumé. Instead, we will counsel you through the three most significant errors that candidates make on their résumés.

1. Lengthy résumés
2. Unclear listings of education and work experience
3. Too much personal information

Error #1. Lengthy Résumés

The single greatest factor that results in your typical "Dear John" rejection letter has nothing to do with your education, qualifications, or experience. The most damaging action that can provide that immediate knockout punch is a *lengthy résumé*.

Résumés should be limited to two pages even if you've held fifteen positions of increasing responsibility over thirty years. Why the concern with length? First, lengthy résumés are a surefire tip-off to your age. If you are in your late fifties or early sixties but look and act forty, you want the opportunity to get in front of a potential employer to show off your youthful outlook and appearance.

Forget all the EEO laws and preaching about hiring older workers. Many employers still shy away from anyone over fifty because there's a significant pool of younger, qualified candidates who don't command high salaries.

———— ❖ ————

MISCONCEPTION

Your résumé is the best sales tool available in the quest to get a job.

REALITY

The only objective of a résumé is to attract attention. Selling yourself should be left for the personal interview.

———— ❖ ————

Second, lengthy résumés are difficult to handle and track when they have to be reproduced or faxed. For example, in response to an employment ad, we received a seven-page résumé from a senior executive in a food-processing company. Since a great sense of urgency existed, my instructions were to fax all appropriate résumés to my client immediately. To fax the seven-pager, we had to remove the staple, and we continually found ourselves mixing up the pages with other résumés that only had one or two pages. Finally, in frustration, my assistant questioned the necessity of sending the discourse since our fax could only feed ten sheets for each transmission. Her comment: "If we eliminate this short story, I will only have to make one transmission."

After carefully thinking about it and reviewing the résumé again, this candidate didn't survive the cut. With the seven-page résumé, it was easy to pinpoint at least a few disqualifying factors because there was so much information to choose from. If it takes more than two pages to list your credentials, you are setting yourself up for failure.

The rule is simple. If it takes more than one stamp to mail your résumé, you're overselling on first contact.

Error #2. Unclear Listings of Education and Work Experience

EDUCATION

Incorrectly listing education credentials creates confusion and raises questions about the validity of your degree. It is critical that you include your specific degree and year of graduation when listing colleges or universities. If you only provide the names of schools

———— ❖ ————

MISCONCEPTION

*The more colleges you list, the better your chances of
impressing a potential employer.*

REALITY

*Listing every course you took and college you attended can
create the perception that you have a difficult
time completing what you start.*

———— ❖ ————

without this important information, most recruiters and personnel people will make the assumption that you did not earn a degree. Examine the following listing from a résumé.

EDUCATION:

1971–73   University of Miami—
           Mechanical Engineering
1967–68   Florida State University—
           Engineering
1964–65   University of Central Florida

Now, consider these questions:

1. Did the individual earn a degree?
2. Did he or she really graduate in 1973?
3. Why did this person attend three schools?

Most recruiters know this format is frequently used by people attempting to hide the fact that they never received a degree. If you have a degree, spell out the details. If it took you several colleges and multiple tries to complete your education, just list the final school, your degree, and the date. Changing colleges can send a message of instability and difficulty in adjusting, particularly if you have a record of frequent job changes. To ensure that your education credentials are not misinterpreted, just state the facts.

EDUCATION:

University of Miami, BS—
Mechanical Engineering, 1973

Remember, the résumé is not an employment application that charts your educational path. It's like that golf saying, "They don't draw pictures on the score card; all you see is the final number."

---------------- ❖ ----------------

MISCONCEPTION

If you had great grades in college, this fact will impress potential employers even if you graduated twenty years ago.

REALITY

The further along in years, the less important is your actual performance in college. Save that space for more important business accomplishments.

---------------- ❖ ----------------

However, if specific questions are asked about your education on an application or during an interview, you must be open and honest about your sojourn.

Also, if you think your age will hinder your chances of getting a job, take a chance by only listing the college and the degree, leaving off the year you graduated. This may open a door that would have otherwise been closed by your age.

Limit the education section to critical information. Who really cares if you graduated with high honors twenty-five years ago? The longer you are out of school, the less important the specifics of your performance in the classroom. Stressing academics can take away valuable space that should be dedicated to your work history and experience.

Finally, if you do not have a degree, it may be best to leave the EDUCATION heading off your résumé. This action focuses the employer's attention on positives such as your accomplishments while neutralizing the fact that you may not have a formal education.

WORK EXPERIENCE

Because of mergers and acquisitions, many job hunters have trouble developing work history descriptions. It is highly possible for someone to hold the same position for ten years while having four different employers who bought the company during that period. Without an explanation, that track record could mislead the reader into thinking, "This person is a job hopper."

———————— ❖ ————————

MISCONCEPTION

The best way to attract attention is to include the unique approaches you've used to accomplish an objective.

REALITY

*Your résumé should only include **what** you have done, not **how** you did it. Too much detail can highlight contrasting management styles.*

———————— ❖ ————————

Also, when smaller companies are purchased by bigger ones, titles often change. Therefore, a vice-president in a $50M company might receive the new title of general manager in a $100M division of a larger corporation but still have the same responsibilities. Same job, different title.

To alleviate this dilemma, stay with your most recent job title and follow this approach:

1980–Present DIRECTOR OF SALES,
              Industrial Products

ABC Corporation
   (Acquired in 1988)

DFG Corporation
   (Acquired in 1985)

XYZ Company
   (Merged in 1983)

This listing will not only show your stability but also your ability to survive several transactions.

Another point of contention is supplying irrelevant and confusing information in your work history. If you were to read the résumé of a notable athlete like Bo Jackson, you would admire a list of his awards and accomplishments, for example, Rookie of the Year, MVP, and leading rusher. What you would not see is a play-by-play summary describing how he reached these pinnacles. That would take a book, and, in fact, it did.

---------------- ❖ ----------------

MISCONCEPTION

Providing detailed personal information on the résumé can be a good hook to explore common grounds with a potential employer.

REALITY

By including too much personal information, you run the risk of hitting a sore spot in the reader's own life.

---------------- ❖ ----------------

List your accomplishments but hold back on the HOWs. Save them for the interview.

Take the following description by Michael, a quality assurance manager, who attempted to package his accomplishment of reducing customer returns by 20 percent.

In a little less than 15 months, I held meetings with my people to insure they rejected every part that was out of spec. This action insured good parts went out the door and cut our return rate by 20%.

A shrewd manager would tear this description apart as a weak approach to address the real issue. "Why are they making bad parts in the first place?"

Michael would be better off restating the accomplishment as it benefited his employer.

Instituted a Q.A. program that reduced customer returns by 20% resulting in a $250,000 cost savings in only 15 months.

This statement will raise the reader's curiosity. "How did he do it?" Plus, it doesn't leave room for a comparison of management styles. Accomplishments, not approaches, get you an invitation to the tryout.

Error #3. Too Much Personal Information

How do you think the following write-up under the heading of PERSONAL INFORMATION would be received by an individual who recently went through a difficult divorce?

Happily married to a wonderful wife with three lovely children.

This description is commonplace. Sure, you should be proud of a happy and stable home life, but displaying this information to somebody on the opposite end of the spectrum could be disastrous. If a solid home front is a critical job requirement, the issue will come up soon enough in an interview.

The same scenario holds true if you belong to certain organizations, whether religious, political, or professional. A chauvinistic manager who reads "Regional director for the National Organization of Women (NOW)" might get intimidated and pass you by.

Again, the safest approach is to stick to the facts and surgically remove any information that could be misinterpreted by a reviewer. You may wish to forgo the personal section in favor of devoting more space to your work history and accomplishments.

Finally, if you've been a job hopper who's held fifteen jobs in the past twenty years, I have two recommendations. First, forget using a résumé and concentrate on developing a great letter of introduction that could get you in the door. Like colleges that have minimum entrance requirements on SAT scores, many employers will disqualify candidates on work histories alone. Second, if you have problems securing and keeping employment in a specific field, such as sales or accounting, maybe it's time to try your hand at another discipline.

CHAPTER 6

When in Doubt . . .
Play by the Rules

The classified ad in the Sunday help-wanted section clearly states:

Forward résumé and salary history to:
Christina Martin, Human Resource Director
No phone calls, please

In an effort to head off the crowd and differentiate yourself should you:

- Ignore the instructions and contact Christina directly?
- Secure the fax number of the company and wire your credentials?
- Send your résumé through a contact who works for the employer?
- Omit your salary history if you don't know the pay range for the advertised position?

———————— ❖ ————————

MISCONCEPTION

Making direct phone contact with a hiring executive usually results in an interview.

REALITY

Making direct contact with a busy executive more often hurts than helps your chances for an interview.

———————— ❖ ————————

These are certainly tough questions that pass through every job hunter's mind at one time or another. Sometimes breaking the rules gives you an edge. Other times, breaking the rules alienates the receiver and eliminates you from the competition.

How your differentiated actions will be received by the people on the other end is the unknown element of this predicament. Will they be impressed by your aggressiveness or irritated by your outright violation of specific instructions? When there are many unknown variables, such as the personality of the recipient and his or her priorities, the safest policy is to play by the rules.

To help you understand the impact of breaking the rules, let's take a behind-the-scenes look at how your actions could be perceived by a potential employer.

Making Direct Contact

We ran an ad in a trade journal for a client who was planning to replace his director of sales. Since the current director was unaware of the pending separation, every effort was made to protect the identity of the client. The ad clearly stated the directions for responding with a bold warning that phone calls would not be accepted. Early on a Monday morning, before the coffee had a chance to brew, our office received a rude call asking for more specifics on the job. Since my staff wasn't involved with this client, they were unable to give any details to the young woman caller. However, after a lot of badgering, one assistant gave our fax number just to get her off the phone. Twenty minutes later, her résumé came in over the fax. Within an hour, a very polite rejection letter was on its way to her home.

---------------- ❖ ----------------

MISCONCEPTION

*Faxing is one of the fastest ways to get your résumé on
potential employers' desks.*

REALITY

*Over 50 percent of all unsolicited faxes never reach the
desks of the intended recipients.*

---------------- ❖ ----------------

The important thing you need to understand is that responding to your calls and correspondence is a very low priority for busy executives. Unexpected calls that get through secretaries or assistants because they are targeted before 8 A.M. or after 5 P.M. more often irritate than impress the receiver.

There is a very thin line between being assertive and being obnoxious. Unfortunately, this is a subjective determination totally dependent on the recipient's state of mind at the instant of contact. You have no control over how someone feels when he or she first glances at your credentials or hears your voice on the phone.

Faxing Unsolicited Information

In addition to alienating someone with an unexpected phone call, unsolicited fax transmissions can also be distracting, creating a poor first impression.

Most companies keep their fax machines unmanned in a central location. Therefore, it is highly probable that your transmission could get lost or misplaced with other faxes. It is not uncommon for a mailroom attendant to have specific instructions to treat unsolicited résumés as junk mail. The same may be true of faxes. So, to determine if your fax reached its destination, you'd have to call a person you don't know, who may have more important tasks than tracking down your fax. You need to keep a realistic perspective on the willingness of a prospective employer to take your call or respond to your information.

---------------- ❖ ----------------

MISCONCEPTION

Omitting your salary history when it is requested will result in a follow-up call.

REALITY

Not giving your salary history when requested is more often interpreted as a negative factor.

---------------- ❖ ----------------

From a pure appearance standpoint, you should be aware that fax paper is thin and slick and has a tendency to curl, making it hard to handle. Also, many dark papers and type styles smudge and distort when transmitted over a fax. This can distort your professional first impression. Be assured, most potential employers will not ask you to resubmit if they can't read your name. Finally, your credentials might have to be reviewed by managers in other locations. It's impossible to fax a fax and maintain a quality appearance. To get your résumé into shape, someone will have to make a special effort to copy your fax. That means extra work and trouble, which can result in a quick trip to the waste barrel.

Since you can't be on the receiving end to ensure a quality transmission to the appropriate people, sending an unsolicited fax is not likely to result in a favorable response.

Sending Your Paperwork Through a Contact

Circumventing the crowds by submitting your credentials with a friend or an associate can help or hurt. In our networking section in Chapter 7, we discuss in detail the pitfalls of getting introduced by the wrong person. If you have a good contact, it may be worthwhile to consider breaking the rules.

Omitting Salary History

Many job seekers wrestle with this decision all the time because they fear this one piece of information that can immediately cut them from the competition. Sometimes a salary that is too low can give the impression that you're not a performer with high hopes and expectations. On the other hand, too high a salary could be interpreted as a stumbling block if you have solid credentials.

---------- ❖ ----------

MISCONCEPTION

Companies are delighted to recruit candidates who previously made more money with another employer.

REALITY

In today's market companies are reluctant to hire at lower salaries due to the financial and emotional impact on the candidate.

---------- ❖ ----------

In a tough job market, the problem of making too much money at a previous job is a more significant concern since so many highly paid, older executives are on the street. Companies usually cite these logical reasons for bypassing people who would come in for less than 20 percent of their last salary:

- New employees become disenchanted once they see the first check at the lower amount.

- Lower pay will keep them looking for a job instead of concentrating on the one at hand.

- Pressure will be too strong on the home front to maintain their previous standard of living, resulting in a loss of enthusiasm on the job.

- New hires who earned more at a previous employer can infect the attitudes of current employees by complaining about low wages.

If your salary history is out of line with the employer's expectations, be prepared to address these thoughts, which will be running through the employer's mind.

Rather than give the impression that your salary requirements are too lofty for the position, comply with the employer's request and submit salary information. But instead of listing a specific salary like $67,578.23, provide a range with an accompanying statement.

Compensation for the past three years, with incentives and salary, has averaged in the mid $60's.

This kind of input enables you to answer the question while providing flexibility for future compensation discussions. The alternative of not including a salary history may leave the impression that you are making big bucks, particularly if you've had plenty of experience in well-known companies. This could be an eliminating factor in itself.

Playing by the rules during the screening process is the first indication that you can be a compatible team member once you are given a chance to play. Break the rules and you may not survive the cut.

CHAPTER 7

Networking with the Proper Partners

When your income is dependent on making a sale, you learn very quickly that the most important aspect of selling is calling on people who can either influence or make a decision.

A very close analogy exists between selling a product and networking for a job. If you call on the right people, you'll make a sale. If you network with the right partners, you'll get introductions to potential employers. But if you tie up with losers, your image as a viable candidate may suffer.

Do you remember this bit of parental wisdom? "You are judged by the company you keep, and if you associate with losers, you will be judged a loser, too." Welcome to the real world of networking.

——————— ❖ ———————

MISCONCEPTION

Any networking is better than no networking.

REALITY

Networking with the wrong people costs you valuable time, money, and energy.

——————— ❖ ———————

Networking is a broad term used to describe the process of making an important job contact through someone other than yourself. This contact can be made through a friend, family member, business associate, clergy person, recruiter, or anyone else who has the inside track to an opening. Networking can be the most important, readily available device to help you identify opportunities and get your hat thrown in the ring.

The people you chose to be your networking partners wind up being your sales representatives for contacts or companies. Once you begin networking, you will find a number of people who are more than happy to help you with introductions. However, when reality sets in, you'll find there is a big difference between people who are able to help and those who are willing to help.

The point here is to ensure that your associates and friends who volunteer are helping instead of giving lip service. If you are concerned that a networking partner is not presenting your case, ask specific questions that pin down contact names and when they received your credentials. Vague responses signal a blackout in your networking lines. Also, if your sources or connections refuse to take your calls about these matters, you can bet that your credentials are still sitting in the out basket. Good follow-up and a gut feeling will determine if your partner is promoting your case.

Now, let's assume you do have a champion willing to present your qualifications. The following two pitfalls need to be addressed before you join forces.

———— ❖ ————

MISCONCEPTION

Most people are only too happy to provide you with an introduction.

REALITY

There is a significant difference between being able to help and actually helping. Many individuals are too timid to provide introductions.

———— ❖ ————

Picking the Wrong Networking Partner

Just like it was yesterday, I remember my first networking experience trying to solicit a sales contact. An
engineer, Rob, who was associated with the corporate
quality group of my employer, volunteered the name
of a man he described as a personal friend who was
the purchasing director at a potential customer. Rob
told me to be sure I mentioned his name when setting
up an appointment. Being a naïve sales rep, I didn't
question Rob's relationship with the customer and made
the call.

To my surprise, the purchasing director didn't recall Rob at all. Finally, out of desperation, I mentioned
that Rob knew him from the Plastics Association. That
comment jogged the director's memory. "Yeah! Now I
know who you're talkin' about. He's the balding idiot
that never shuts his mouth." The customer unfortunately described Rob perfectly, and because I thought
Rob was a mover and a shaker, I lost the respect of the
account and never got in the door.

After that embarrassing experience, I always asked
a lot of questions and did significant research on any
person who offered networking assistance. Networking
with the wrong person can cost you valuable time,
money, and, more important, respect. The adage,
"Consider the source," applies directly to networking.
Your networking partners must be held in high esteem
by the people making the hiring decisions. Having your
résumé presented to a marketing manager by a salesperson who is 40 percent behind quota will do little to
push your chances of securing an invitation to discuss
your qualifications.

---------------- ❖ ----------------

MISCONCEPTION

You will be judged on your merits, not by the person who provides the contact.

REALITY

You are judged by the company you keep. A poor networking partner will reflect negatively on your stature.

---------------- ❖ ----------------

Getting Caught in a Political Squeeze

Another hazardous aspect of networking involves getting swept up in company politics. You must be careful not to alienate any staff people who justify their existence through recruiting. This can result in an early exit from consideration.

Mary previously worked for Jim as a market researcher for ten years before he accepted a position with another company. When Mary found out her current position was being eliminated, she contacted Jim at his new company and inquired about possible opportunities. To Mary's delight, Jim informed her that he recently submitted an open job requisition to personnel for a research position that would match her talents. At Jim's suggestion, she forwarded a copy of her résumé to the personnel director.

What Mary didn't know was that the day her résumé arrived, the personnel manager was meeting with the CEO on a staffing plan that included Jim's not-yet-approved requisition. Since Jim was the new kid on the block, the CEO instructed the personnel manager to seek additional justification for the new research position. Because Jim didn't have a track record, this would be an excellent test of his management prowess.

When the personnel manager arrived back at his office, he noticed Mary's unsolicited résumé on his desk. He was surprised by the audacity of Jim to discuss a proposed position with someone outside of the company. Irate, the personnel manager commented to his assistant, "I'll teach Jim that no requisition is approved until I sign off on it first." Later on that week the personnel manager convinced the CEO that it was not necessary to fund the research position.

What about Mary? Well, she was left out in the cold because she unexpectedly walked onto the field of a hard-hitting, political football game.

There's no substitute for doing your homework when it comes to networking. Investigate your networking partners and ask questions about the political environment of a potential employer.

One final thought: Make sure that bragging neighbor, who is senior vice-president of "everything," really isn't an assistant to the assistant of the data processing manager. A ten-second phone call to his employer's switchboard confirming his title may be one of the best investments you make during your search.

CHAPTER 8

Recruiting the Right
Employment Agency

All employment agencies are not created equal.

Search firms, headhunters, employment agencies, and independent recruiters can be wonderful vehicles for entries into hiring companies. However, like our discussion about networking, you have to know who, how, and when to call on the services of an independent employment firm.

Remember, the employer is king and you have to follow his wishes regarding the use of outside agencies. Some companies are very dependent on agencies while others use agencies only as a last resort when a direct approach fails to produce viable candidates.

———————— ❖ ————————

MISCONCEPTION

All employment agencies are alike.

REALITY

There are significant differences in the ways agencies operate.

———————— ❖ ————————

Whatever the case, before you proceed, you need to determine the type or types of agencies that will provide the best opportunity to get you in the door.

Executive Search Firms—Fees Paid Up Front

This type of agency is most often contracted if there's a shortage of specific skills, if confidentiality is critical, or if a current employee is headed for termination.

Search firms get paid even if positions remain unfilled. Their fees are based on a percentage of the estimated starting salary. Traditionally, a 30 percent fee is awarded for high-level positions. At a glance, these fees may seem hefty. However, when you consider it may take 100 phone calls, 30 preliminary phone interviews, and 40 reference checks before two good candidates can be identified, the cost is justifiable.

The major pressure on search firms is to produce viable candidates, not necessarily to make placements. It is not uncommon for search firms to present several candidates and have all of them rejected by the contracting company. Search firms that have an exclusive, fee-paid contract may be your best avenue into new companies when your background has gray areas or if you have a history of frequent job changes.

Commission-Paid Recruiters

These agencies work on a sliding commission basis only if a placement is made. This fee can reach upward of 35 percent of the starting salary for high-paying positions. Unlike fee-paid search firms that customarily get paid up front, commissioned recruiters

———————— ❖ ————————

MISCONCEPTION

To get the attention of a first-class executive search firm, you must be currently employed in a high-paying job.

REALITY

Search firms are probably your best avenue when you are unemployed and looking to secure a top position.

———————— ❖ ————————

are compensated fifteen to thirty days after the candidate is hired. These agencies will also provide certain guarantees on placements and will often replace candidates at no cost if they quit within six months.

Commissioned agencies are most frequently called recruiters and consultants. Sometimes they have exclusive assignments, but it is more common for vacancies to be spread among several recruiters in an effort to blanket the market in search for the best candidates.

Search firms and commissioned recruiters have different levels of motivation. Search firms that are more exclusive have a different agenda than recruiting agencies that often compete with several other agencies for the same opening. Therefore, recruiters may only get a limited number of chances to produce good candidates. So, unless they lack viable candidates, commissioned recruiters will not present individuals who are hard to sell.

Three factors can make you a hard sell, limiting a recruiter's ability to place you with a client successfully.

1. Being unemployed
2. Lacking the specified education
3. Changing jobs frequently

Being unemployed.
Everyone wants what they can't have. The fact that your present employer still keeps you around provides justification for your credentials. No personnel manager will ever be called on the carpet for a sloppy search if the new hire was working for another company at the time of employment.

---------- ❖ ----------

MISCONCEPTION

*If you are unemployed, recruiters will have empathy and
present your credentials before those of someone
who is working.*

REALITY

*Being unemployed makes you a harder sell and a more risky
placement than a person who is gainfully employed.*

---------- ❖ ----------

On the other hand, hiring an individual who is out of work carries a certain risk—the first question a CEO will ask when a new employee doesn't make the grade is "Why the hell did we hire someone that another company got rid of?" Given the choice, companies will hire a candidate who is working over another who is unemployed.

Lacking the specified education.
Like being unemployed, not possessing the level of education required in the job description also creates a liability that may be difficult to overcome.

Foreign ownership in this country is placing greater emphasis on education. You can have terrific experience and a great background, but if you don't meet the educational requirements, you won't have much of a chance. So, when recruiters tell you they'll push for a position even though you don't have the education, watch their noses real closely to see if they're growing. The sell may be too tough.

Changing jobs frequently.
Job hoppers only land positions when openings abound or they possess specific skills that employers desperately need. Once job hoppers get laid off in a competitive market, their stock drops off the board, and recruiters won't waste time presenting them. If you have a record of frequent job changes, don't rely solely on agencies to provide your introductions.

Now, whether you decide to go with an executive search firm or a recruiter, you must ask yourself two more questions. First, should I use a specialized or general agency? Second, should I work with one or many agencies?

———————— ❖ ————————

MISCONCEPTION

It is best to work with many different agencies so that a spirit of competition will develop to place you in a job.

REALITY

Working with too many agencies can result in crossed wires and conflicts.

———————— ❖ ————————

Specialized vs. General Agencies

Many agencies specialize in placements by job function instead of industries. For example, several national franchises focus on only recruiting sales candidates. Their assignments cross industry boundaries, and they are most often called upon by employers when the market is tight for talent. These firms best suit individuals who have skills that can be translated from one industry to another.

Conversely, general agencies can still function within one industry or market but differ from specialists in that they help to locate candidates for positions ranging from a plant manager to a VP of sales. These firms usually have better, in-depth relationships with their customers because of repeat business and intimate knowledge of the customers' operations. Many general agencies also offer reduced commission structures for good clients and often have an inside track on up-and-coming positions. If your skills are highly technical or slanted to one industry, a general agency with good customer contacts may be your best ally.

Single Vs. Multiple Agencies

The advantage of using one agency solely is that working with one firm helps in developing a mutually beneficial relationship. Agencies tend to work harder when they have your loyalty. The disadvantage of using one agency is possibly missing an opportunity outside that agency's listings. However, like real estate brokers, most agencies often share both candidates and openings in the hope of being the agency of record and the agency that collects the fee.

A word of caution if you choose to work with multiple agencies: Be up front with the representatives and tell them about your game plan. You should also keep them appraised of the companies you have contacted through classified ads, networking with associates, or dealing with other recruiters. Nothing is more frustrating and embarrassing to an agency than having your credentials show up on the client's desk from a competing recruiter. In addition to alienating the agency, when your résumé arrives from several recruiters, the client's perception of you as a prized candidate will be weakened.

Selecting an agency requires time and research to determine which one will best fit your needs. Talk to personnel managers, associates, and friends to get their recommendations on good performers in your field.

In a tough market, the employer is king. Having the right agency could get you a special invitation to the castle.

CHAPTER 9

Responding to Blind Ads
with Your Eyes Open

Blind employment ads ask you to reply to a box number or an agency. In other words, the name of the company is withheld. But the perception that blind ads are used only to protect the identity of a hiring company is not always true.

Sometimes these ads are placed to check the availability of qualified employees working for the competition. Blind ads are also used to identify current employees who might be on the prowl. For this reason, replying to a blind ad when you are gainfully employed is dangerous.

MISCONCEPTION

The only purpose of a blind ad is to protect the advertiser.

REALITY

Blind ads can be used to gauge market activity and determine if current employees are looking for new opportunities.

Traditionally, blind ads draw weak responses from a quality and qualifications standpoint. Handwritten envelopes, poorly written cover letters, and disorganized résumés are the rule rather than the exception.

In good economic times, when a large percentage of the people looking for new jobs are still employed, it is rare for a blind ad to produce viable candidates. But if you are unemployed, there is no real risk in replying. The key is to do it right.

As I stated, employers don't hold high expectations for the responses to blind ads. So if you can respond in a professional manner, your paperwork will stand out in the crowd.

Use a safe salutation. When writing to the recipient, avoid addressing your correspondence with "Gentlemen," "Madam," "Sir," or "Ms." The person could be a personnel manager, VP of engineering, or even president of a recruiting company.

I have read over ten thousand responses to blind ads, and there are two safe ways to address the correspondence.

April 15, 1991

To Whom It May Concern:

   or

April 15, 1991

To: Box #1234
Re: Solicitation for a Plant Manager

Both these approaches are factual and don't make any incorrect assumptions.

MISCONCEPTION

Responding to a blind ad shows that you are desperate.

REALITY

A careful, well-orchestrated response to a blind ad will give the impression that you are a professional with a serious approach to finding a job.

Don't oversell. Since you are responding to a blind ad, try not to oversell yourself by supplying too much information. You don't want the prospective employer to think you're desperate. When you supply bits of information, you have a better chance of piquing the interest of the advertiser. Personal letters that briefly state your reason for responding to a blind ad, accompanied by a short description of your work history without disclosing your employers, may be just what you need to flush out the advertiser.

Another approach that can be used effectively to flush out the hiring company, without revealing your name, is to contract a private outplacement firm to act as an intermediary. A credible outplacement firm can send a short letter and synopsis of your background and suggest that the employer respond with reference to a file number. The most attractive part of this process to the potential employer . . . *no fee is involved.*

A typical cover letter from a third party might have the following introduction:

April 15, 1991

To Whom It May Concern:

We read about your position for a plant manager with much interest. We have both good news and bad news for you. The good news is we have a candidate who meets all your qualifications and is available with *no placement fee.* The bad news is we cannot reveal the candidate's name. If you wish to meet with this individual, please contact us and refer to file #PM-234.

When an employer sees a short list of the right qualifications provided by a professional agency at no cost, you can be assured the letter will get attention. The out-of-pocket cost for such services usually runs between $75–$150/hour. It may be a worthwhile investment to consider. Because of this approach, our company has successfully placed individuals who were about to lose positions to downsizing.

One final note or word of caution on blind ads: It is not uncommon for a company to run two or maybe three blind ads in the same newspaper with slightly different qualifications to see who is applying for every position. We keep a file of all our respondents, and you'd be amazed at the stable of résumés some people have to fit whatever job is advertised. We had one person who responded to fifteen blind ads in the last five years with ten different cover letters and five convertible résumés.

The rule here is to limit your response to those opportunities that fit your qualifications while being consistent with your approach. You never know when the employers behind the masks will compare notes.

CHAPTER 10

The Phone Only Rings Once for Successful Candidates

Remember the critical stage in the movie that produced the famous line, *"E.T., phone home."* The fate of an entire planet depended on that one critical link: E.T. getting the message and phoning home.

Each time the phone rings when you're looking for work, it should bring you new hope that a potential employer has taken notice of your qualifications and is ready to invite you to the tryout.

Yet so many job seekers fail to recognize the importance of being accessible while ensuring their phone gets answered in a professional manner. Time and time again, candidates are eliminated from the competition because they can't be reached. Or, even worse, when they are reached, they create a poor impression that turns off recruiters.

—————————— ❖ ——————————

MISCONCEPTION

If you have great credentials, potential employers will keep calling if they can't reach you on the first couple of attempts.

REALITY

With time constraints and many qualified candidates available, a recruiter will seldom make more than two attempts to reach you.

—————————— ❖ ——————————

Over the years, I have disqualified somewhere between fifty and seventy-five potential candidates because of the rude and terse manner in which their spouse or children answered the phone. During that same period it's also possible that an additional twenty-five to fifty candidates never received my messages regarding an employment opportunity.

The following is a description of three actions that can sour potential employers after they've phoned your home.

1. *An unattended phone.*

The assumption most recruiters make is that your quest to find a job is important enough to ensure your availability eighteen hours a day. Time zone differences, international travel, and other factors could result in that important phone call coming any time between six A.M. and eleven P.M.

Also, most recruiters have several candidates to screen with the objective of inviting two for on-site interviews. They may try once or even twice to reach you, but after the second attempt, your paperwork will be relegated to the back burner if other screening calls produce viable candidates. The sad part about this scenario is that both you and the potential employer may be missing out on a beneficial marriage.

And by the way, busy signals caused by that teenage daughter or son talking to friends for hours on end can be just as damaging as an unattended phone. Call waiting, then, may be a worthwhile investment if you have a household with teenagers. Time constraints and the abundance of qualified candidates will preclude recruiters from trying to reach you over and over again.

———————— ❖ ————————

MISCONCEPTION

*Off-the-wall messages on your answering machine
demonstrate your creativity.*

REALITY

*Offbeat recordings, as clever as you may think they are, can
be irritating and offensive.*

———————— ❖ ————————

Remember, the phone number you provide on your résumé must be answered by the fourth ring either by a responsible person or an answering machine with a good, solid message.

2. *Unprofessional or emotional answering-machine recordings.*

> "Hi! I'm Kathy! I'm Billy! And these are our two little cowgirls, Kerri and Tara . . ."

Give me a break! I actually heard a family sing this message. Number one, they couldn't carry a tune, and number two, since Billy was being considered to head a tough union shop in a metal-fabricating plant, well . . . I couldn't tell you how the song ended.

Recorded messages should sound clear, short, and professional. If you're the one looking for work, your voice should be on the recording, not your five-year-old son with his dog barking in the background. The longer your recorded instructions, the more likely a potential employer will hear something offensive that could result in a hang-up.

3. *Rude and terse family members.*

The following dialogue actually occurred between a CEO and the wife of a manager he was looking to hire for a top-level position in a plastics-molding company.

Keep in mind, this woman would have to accompany her husband to outings and major trade association meetings as a representative of the company.

---------------- ❖ ----------------

MISCONCEPTION

Family members that take your calls have no impact on the caller's perception of you.

REALITY

Especially in top positions, the manner in which your family takes your calls can have a significant impact on your employer's perception of you.

---------------- ❖ ----------------

CEO: Hello . . . Is Mr. Kubert there?
WIFE: I don't know where he is, but just hold
         on . . . Will you kids shut the hell up!
         I'm trying to take a damn message. I
         said, SHUT UP."
CEO: *Click!*

That's right—the CEO hung up. The wife's extreme demeanor and indifference crushed any chances her husband had of landing the position. Was this fair to the candidate? Probably not, but in the real world, your messenger can be your only link with the employer.

In addition, children, particularly teenagers, can blow your chances for an invitation by answering the phone with teenage slang: "Like, hi . . . the dude's not in and I don't know when he'll be back. I think he's workin' or somethin'."

Don't be surprised if a potential employer evaluates your character based on your children's behavior. As the saying goes, "The apple doesn't fall too far from the tree." Therefore, make every attempt to either train your children how to take these important calls, or keep them away from the phone.

A few final points on attending and answering the phone. It's impressive when the person taking the message acts like the call is not only important but expected. To set this kind of tone, have the message taker repeat the caller's name, company, phone number, and message. Showing appreciation for the call with a thank you goes a long way toward creating a positive, lasting impression.

Remember, in high-level positions where you will be a visible representative in the community, your spouse and family are all part of a package deal. A polite, well-spoken family will increase your chances of surviving the cut. So, take time out with family members to explain the importance of your calls and demonstrate how to take a message. Sometimes it's even helpful to prepare a small printed list that contains critical information, such as the caller's name, the company, the phone number, and the best time to return the call. Keep it right by the phone.

In the end, if you don't feel you can present that professional, polished image at home, it is recommended that you make a small investment in an independent answering service.

You can't get a tryout if you never get the call. And please, please, make certain the person taking your messages gets the caller's name right. I just hate being called Mr. Durrfey.

PART II

How to Shine During the Tryout

CHAPTER 11

The Interview—Your Tryout
for the Team

Be yourself. That's the best piece of advice I can offer when you approach an interview.

This approach and style will provide you with an edge over the competition. An interview is a personal meeting used to explore common ground between you and the employer. It is during this time frame that both parties look for a common chemistry that will produce a good working relationship.

Putting on airs or acting or trying to be someone other than yourself will place a tremendous strain on both you and the interviewer. Eventually, no matter how hard you try, your true character traits will surface. This will only cause tension brought on by the mixed signals you were sending in the first place.

———— ❖ ————

MISCONCEPTION

It is best to rehearse the responses to possible questions from an interviewer.

REALITY

BE YOURSELF!

———— ❖ ————

As we have discussed, this book's focus is on actions that will hurt your chances of making the team versus planning a structured approach to finding a job. To have a successful venture on the employer's playing field, several actions need to be addressed to sensitize yourself during the interview process.

First, you need to prepare and demonstrate that you care enough about the opportunity to have taken the liberty of researching the company. Time is a precious commodity, and the minutes taken by a busy executive to bring you up to speed will detract from valuable interview time.

Next, you must look presentable. Appearances are important. You need not look like a model out of *GQ* or *Vogue*. Just make sure your clothes are neat, tailored, and appropriate for the position you are seeking.

When you arrive for your appointment, tune in to the needs of not only the people you will be interviewing with, but also others, such as receptionists and secretaries who are looking for warm attention. These "silent" interviewers may have more input than you think.

Finally, ask good questions that relate to the job, its responsibilities, and how it fits into the overall corporate strategy. Good questions, not brilliant answers, will clearly reveal your level of interest and understanding for the position.

In the following chapters, we will walk you through these and other actions that could contribute to a short tryout.

CHAPTER 12

Preparing for the Tryout

Like an athlete preparing for an event, you have to get in shape before the interview. This requires both physical and mental preparation.

Preparing Physically for the Interview

It seems obvious, but you must ensure that your clothes and appearance will not negatively impact on the individuals who will be part of the interview process.

That's not to suggest you look and dress like a movie star. However, it's recommended that you make sure your clothes fit and are appropriate for the audience.

---- ❖ ----

MISCONCEPTION

Interviewers will excuse a shabby appearance because they know you are unemployed.

REALITY

Sloppy dress makes a poor first impression that is hard to overcome, even if you interview well.

---- ❖ ----

It's understandable that being unemployed creates certain mental and financial pressures that often result in stress-related eating disorders. Translated: You put on a few extra pounds in the wrong places.

Nothing is more distracting than to sit for an hour and look at someone dressed in a suit that is three sizes too small. Shirts that don't button at the collar and belts that are out to the last hole signal that one small facet of your life is out of control.

I remember one time when a slightly overweight gentleman came into my office for a screening interview. When he sat down, the first thing I noticed was his belly protruding between his shirt buttons. If you asked me today what I remembered most about this candidate, the exposed belly would come to mind. His poor appearance detracted from anything of substance he had to say.

If your clothes don't fit, either attempt to lose the weight or purchase new clothes that will do your physique some justice. The objective is not to leave the employer with the impression that you are a snazzy dresser but to neutralize your appearance so that it doesn't negatively affect the potential employer's perception of you. I have yet to see an employer hire someone because of his or her spiffy appearance, but many candidates have been disqualified because of shabby or poorly fitted clothing.

A final thought on dressing for the occasion. Keep track of the outfits you wear to each interview. Try to vary your wardrobe when the interview process requires multiple visits to the same office. Wearing the same maroon sports coat on three successive interviews

———— ❖ ————

MISCONCEPTION

When you have to travel three hours to an interview, the people you meet will understand if you yawn.

REALITY

Regardless of the justification, yawning is rude and can signal to an employer that you are bored or disinterested.

———— ❖ ————

might lead the company to think you only have one coat—that you're really down on your luck and desperate for any job. Borrow an extra coat if you have to. Just make sure it fits.

Preparing Mentally for the Interview

To be ready mentally for the tryout, make sure you are:

- On time
- Rested and alert
- Well versed on the company

Being on time for the interview.

A late arrival shows disrespect, disorganization, a poor perspective, and immaturity.

Consider this plight. You're conducting screening interviews for a Midwest sales representative in a major hotel at Chicago's O'Hare Airport. You set your schedule to interview four candidates starting at 9 A.M. with two hours allotted for each. You have a 6 P.M. flight back to New York. Then the first candidate doesn't arrive until 10:15. His excuse: "Unbelievably heavy traffic." You are disturbed because you will be in a catch-up mode for the balance of the day. What kind of a review would you give the late candidate? A sales candidate who is over fifteen minutes late without notice will almost always be disqualified, regardless of the excuse.

If you know you are going to be late because of unforeseen circumstances, call and give the interviewer the option of having you come ahead or scheduling you for another date.

---------- ❖ ----------

MISCONCEPTION

You can never overprepare for an interview.

REALITY

Too much information can be dangerous, particularly if it leads to in-depth discussions out of your area of expertise.

---------- ❖ ----------

Being rested and alert.

Driving four hours to an interview through traffic and rain will drain anyone's energy. You should attempt to set your schedule so the travel time to an interview is no more than one hour. You will look, feel, and perform better.

It is also very impressive when a company finds out you booked yourself into a local hotel the night before, ensuring that you arrive on time and alert. This action shows you're not afraid to travel, you plan ahead, and you care about the interview. It is a sign of respect and professionalism.

Researching the company.

A company's primary objective during an interview is to learn about your personality and talents. The more time the interviewer uses to explain the company's background and products, the less time you have to make an impression.

The following background questions can knock you out of the running if you ask them during the early stages of the interview.

- "So what do you guys make here?"
- "Gee, until you called, I never heard of your company. Are you people a division of another company or something?"

There's the door. Any candidate who doesn't take the time to find out at least a little about the company shows a lack of initiative and concern.

---------------- ❖ ----------------

MISCONCEPTION

Companies are reluctant to share financial and sales histories until they confirm that an individual is a viable candidate.

REALITY

Most astute executives expect that management candidates will probe at the appropriate time for information that is important to assess the opportunity.

---------------- ❖ ----------------

At a minimum, you should find out the following about a potential employer:

1. Products or services
2. Markets
3. Annual sales
4. Number of employees
5. Perception in the market
6. Potential for a buyout or merger

Armed with this information gathered from annual reports, industrial directories, and conversations with associates, you will be able to ask more pertinent and intelligent questions during the interview.

You should also be aware of the downside to overpreparing for an interview. Take the case of Dolores, a candidate for a market analyst position in a large chemical company. Since Dolores had a degree in accounting, she felt right at home dissecting the annual report and preparing an extensive list of questions for her interviews.

As part of the process, the last person Dolores met was the comptroller, who had recently been on the hot seat to get inventories under control. Well, you guessed it. Dolores started in on cash flow and inventory questions, irritating the man to the point where he cut the interview short. This top official was taking enough heat from the directors and didn't need additional pressure from a B.S. in accounting who was applying for a $55,000 job in the marketing group. Dolores never survived the final cut because her extensive preparation trapped her into a confrontational discussion.

However, when you are applying for a top-level position where a significant portion of your income will be derived from incentive compensation, tough questions are in order. Just make sure they are asked well into the meeting with the objective of learning about the company's financial and market conditions. At a high level, not asking these questions will raise concern about your street sense because some issues are expected to be addressed.

Being physically and mentally prepared for an interview will help bolster your confidence and self-esteem. When you feel good, you will perform well in the tryout.

CHAPTER 13

Good Questions Are
More Impressive Than
the Right Answers

The way to impress an interviewer is with *insightful questions, not with great answers*. Questions let the interviewer know that you're with the program because you are listening. Also, questions will result in two advantages for you during the interview process.

1. Questions provide you with feedback that can be used to answer future questions.
2. Questions show your level of interest and competence.

---------------- ❖ ----------------

MISCONCEPTION

Employers pay closer attention to your responses than to your questions.

REALITY

Questions demonstrate your aptitude for absorbing the information that is transpiring in the conversation.

---------------- ❖ ----------------

Using Questions to Develop a Data Base

Most interview processes require multiple meetings with individuals from different functional areas. For example, a candidate for a plant manager's position might meet with the CEO, CFO, and the VP of operations. By asking questions about company policies and philosophies, you can gain valuable insight into those factors viewed as sacred cows. If a company is market-driven, you need that information before you can give your insights on how cost-effective manufacturing strategies will make selling the product an easy task.

Questions will also provide valuable background information on the decision makers in the company. Appropriate questions can uncover preferences and attitudes about the position you're interviewing for.

Let's say you're interviewing with a company that is going outside its staff to fill the position. It's prudent to know the sensitivities of the people who were bypassed for the position. You may find that there are several individuals who will try to dissuade you from coming on board, hoping the company will change its mind and reconsider insiders for the position. Then, once you meet with top management, it's perfectly acceptable to air the negative issues that were raised by these individuals. This action will clear the air and provide you with the motivation for the comments of others.

———— ❖ ————

MISCONCEPTION

Too many questions show that you are not comprehending the gist of the conversation.

REALITY

Questions are a sure sign that you are listening and paying close attention to the conversation.

———— ❖ ————

Using Questions to Show Interest and Competence

When decision makers compare notes after your interviews, the ultimate compliment you can receive is that you asked good questions. It is a tribute to your intelligence and genuine interest in the company.

However, to receive this compliment, you must learn how and when to ask the right questions. As easy as it sounds, probing for information without alienating the respondent is an art.

To uncover the facts, you should only ask questions for the sake of learning and not for the sake of asking.

"I see where this company increased sales by 25 percent last year. What a great accomplishment. How did you do it in such a tough market?"

This interest-driven question, asked in a friendly manner, will provide an open-ended response that will afford you valuable information about the person's interests and strengths.

This same question asked in a different manner could be taken as a challenge, irritating the interviewer.

"Did your department make any contributions to the sales increase last year?"

The gut reaction of the respondent, who by the way is interviewing you, may be "None of your business," and the issue will be handled with vague generalities.

———————— ❖ ————————

MISCONCEPTION

It is best to ask questions about benefits and vacation policies early in the process so that the employer knows you are interested in the position.

REALITY

Asking questions about benefits too early in the interview can send the signal that your priorities of getting the job and staying in the competition are out of order.

———————— ❖ ————————

Another important aspect of questioning is the timing. Asking nitty-gritty questions early in an interview can negatively impact the interviewer's perception of your overall management style. Questions that focus on vacation, sick pay, education benefits, and insurance should be saved for final discussions. Broaching these topics any earlier will signal your tendency to "sweat the small stuff" versus "look at the big picture."

It is safe to assume, in most high-level positions, that if you prematurely raise issues like benefits and vacation, it may cause a deal to break down. You should always wait and let the employer raise these issues. Focus your questions on attitudes and strategies. Questions dealing with budgets, staffing, and technology are suitable and necessary for both you and the employer.

To gain some insight into areas you think are important, try using the following nonchallenging phrases as lead-ins.

- "Please explain a little more about that unique strategy."
- "Assuming I come on board, what would be your expectations?"
- "Would you please elaborate a bit more on that interesting point?"
- "What are your feelings on . . ."

Safe, unassuming lead-ins allow the respondent to address a topic comfortably, and you, in turn, extract valuable information.

When you complete your tryout, the employer should know, without doubt, your level of competence and true interest in the position.

One of the best ways to cement the deal and leave a lasting impression is to ask one final question.

"Now that we spent the day together, do you think I am the right person for the position?"

Now on the surface this may appear to be a bold question that puts the interviewers on the spot. But I can assure you if the interviews have gone well, the question will be interpreted as a sure sign of your confidence and interest.

It is to be hoped they'll respond, "If you really want the job!"

CHAPTER 14

Beware of Powerful
Silent Interviewers

Somewhere, lurking quietly in the background of most companies, are silent interviewers who will be asked for their impression of you upon the completion of your tryout. These unassuming yet influential people could be administrators, secretaries, or receptionists in corporate offices.

I learned the value of these silent interviewers the hard way. Many years ago, when I was national sales manager for a plastics company, we needed to add a sales representative in the greater New York City area. Now anyone who has experienced selling in the Big Apple knows you have to be aggressive and thick-skinned to survive in this tough market.

---------- ❖ ----------

MISCONCEPTION

Secretaries are seldom asked for input on job candidates who are going through the interview process.

REALITY

A secretary who has worked for an executive for a number of years has a great deal of influence over his or her decisions.

---------- ❖ ----------

With this criterion in my mind, our company hired Hank, a six-foot-four, 240-pound, imposing individual touted as a great salesperson. We figured if anybody could take the pounding in this market, Hank was our man. But as time passed, we were surprised to discover that Hank lacked both the manners and the personal etiquette expected from a sales professional. He was loud and boisterous, and phrases like "thank you" and "excuse me" didn't exist in his vocabulary. If he couldn't close a deal, he'd point the finger at others within our company. This unacceptable behavior alienated our customer service personnel and created ill will with the customers.

Six months later, we parted ways. Hank just didn't work out. The day we broke ties, my secretary, Dorothy, a quiet and classy woman, came into my office and offered some advice. Dorothy said that she knew Hank wouldn't work out. When I asked how she knew, she commented, "He wasn't a very nice person."

As it turned out, when Hank was being interviewed, Dorothy tried to show him some hospitality only to be totally ignored. She felt Hank had no interest in her because she was "only" a secretary. From that day, Dorothy became my top advisor by silently interviewing each and every candidate who came through the door. Regardless of what I thought, if my silent interviewer didn't have a good feeling, the candidate was out. And by the way, in a three-year period, Dorothy had a perfect record.

———— ❖ ————

MISCONCEPTION

Showing courtesy to individuals not directly involved in the interview is a waste of energy.

REALITY

Being polite to each and every person you meet, regardless of their position, will paint a favorable picture of you as a decent human being.

———— ❖ ————

So keep in mind that individuals who are not pre-conditioned or responsible for hiring can provide excellent, objective input on the character and chemistry of a candidate. The moral: When you're on someone's playing field, you should make a concerted effort to take the time to treat everyone you meet with respect and dignity. That's not to imply that you should act out niceties. But remember to show consideration for others even when they are not directly involved in your interviews.

A lack of common courtesy can really cut your tryout short. Just ask Harry. He was the candidate of choice for the top marketing position with a leading automotive supplier. His experience, track record, and references were ideal. This perfect candidate had the job once the compensation program was worked out.

During the last meeting, Harry asked, or maybe a more appropriate word to use would be *ordered*, the president's assistant to get him a cup of coffee. A short time later, she returned with a lukewarm cup. Rather than swallow it with a smile, Harry complained and made a curt remark. "The executive suite will have its own machine once I come on board."

At that instant the president could see the hurt in his assistant's eyes, and he later excused himself from the room. Outside in the hall, he asked his assistant of ten years if she felt Harry would be a good team player. "I don't really know, but I can tell you one thing, I won't enjoy working with him."

That was the beginning of the end for Harry, who saw his offer slowly slip away. The president politely told him he would have to review their discussions with the board of directors.

Harry's mistreatment of the president's assistant totally wiped out a month of good meetings and interviews.

Unlike Harry, you should respect everyone you meet. Listen, ask questions, and show you care about each person. The same applies for any phone contact with company representatives both before and after the interview. When you complete your rounds, it doesn't hurt to have a silent interviewer in your corner.

For Better or Worse . . . Your Spouse Can Make the Difference

Top-level positions require a commitment not only from you but also from your entire family.

An objective and understanding home support system is critical to the success of any executive. Long hours, constant travel, and tension present situations that family members must understand. When an executive starts getting pressure from home, it won't take long before it manifests itself in poor job performance.

Therefore, for most high-level positions, companies make it a practice to informally interview the spouse of a candidate. Frequently, this interview occurs in a casual setting, such as dinner, but you can be assured that the host and hostess will vigorously compare notes once the evening ends.

---------------- ❖ ----------------

MISCONCEPTION

If you have great qualifications and an excellent track record, your home life will be of no concern to potential employers.

REALITY

Employers are very concerned about the degree of support candidates will receive from family members.

---------------- ❖ ----------------

I've seen several deals fall apart at this late stage because of a spouse's comments made over dinner. One case in particular stands out. Robert and his wife, Susan, had flown to Atlanta to have dinner with the CEO and his girlfriend. The position at stake was VP of finance for a $100M manufacturer of industrial-metal products. Robert came across very well in the interviews, and the management team held him in high regard. The dinner was designed to be more of a social event. In addition, Robert and Susan were using the trip to look at housing since they would have to relocate if all went as expected.

Right after cocktails, Susan started asking the CEO's girlfriend a number of very personal questions.

"Have you ever been married?"

"Are you planning to get married soon?"

"Where did you buy that dress?"

The CEO's date felt pressured and embarrassed. Later that evening, in private, the girlfriend advised the CEO to "keep that awful woman away from me." The following Monday the company instituted a hiring freeze that lasted just long enough to drop Robert from the picture.

Robert had a liability he couldn't control—*his wife.*

During the course of a three-hour dinner with drinks, people cannot hide their true colors. Negative digs or comments from a spouse about travel, long hours, and time away from the family will concern potential employers. Another mistake often made by a

---------------- ❖ ----------------

MISCONCEPTION

Employers are dutifully impressed with spouses who are very focused on their own careers.

REALITY

If your spouse gives the impression that his or her career is more important than yours, it could negatively impact on the company's impression of you.

---------------- ❖ ----------------

spouse is controlling the conversation with his or her own job and career stories. Whoever is picking up the tab for dinner wants to hear about the spouse's support of the applicant, not how he or she is going to get promoted to a new position. Any time the spouse leaves the impression that his or her career is more important than the job seeker's, it will likely result in a knockout blow for the candidate.

However, a positive side to this coin exists. Your spouse can be an asset who helps you land a job. One of the most striking comments I can recall from a reference check was made about a candidate's wife being an asset to her husband and the company.

Executive positions require tremendous understanding from your better half. This kind of support will go a long way in helping you land a position. Therefore, helping your spouse through a potentially uncomfortable situation can be as easy as taking the time to provide background information on the people who will attend the informal meeting.

You should be careful not to overprepare. Stick to social issues like previous homes, the number and ages of children, and inquiries about the local community.

The spouse should always refrain from getting involved in a focused strategy or market discussion, even if he or she can meaningfully add to the conversation. It is critical to ensure your spouse keeps a proper perspective because you're the one looking for the job.

If your spouse is an asset, it is prudent to include him or her in the tryout. But if you are apprehensive that your spouse may create the wrong image or perception, it's best to bow out with a reasonable excuse.

For better or worse, your spouse can have a definite impact on your chances of landing a great position. Just be sure you know where your better half stands.

PART III

Making the Team

CHAPTER 16

Following Up with Interest
and Appreciation

After your tryout, a period of anticipation sets in while
you wait and hope to be extended an opportunity to
join the team.

It is during this period, immediately following your
interview, that it is appropriate and polite to send a
follow-up letter. Often, submitting travel expenses provides a natural vehicle for dropping a note to the key
people you've met.

The cardinal rule on follow-up letters, assuming
you did a respectable job with the interviews, is to
never introduce something new that will expose a different side of your personality.

---------------- ❖ ----------------

MISCONCEPTION

Follow-up letters should be a testimony to how much information you gathered in an interview.

REALITY

Interviewers frown on a recap of the interview in a follow-up letter.

---------------- ❖ ----------------

Probably the single most embarrassing moment in my years of interviewing involved a follow-up letter from Howard, a marketing executive who was working for a prestigious consulting company. I presented him to my client as a level-headed, hard-working person who could step in and make an immediate impact. Then, after two days of successful interviews, a letter arrived at my client's office. It started "I had a startling dream last night that we were at dinner with the board of directors. We were being praised for a wonderful product rollout . . ." This strange and totally offbeat follow-up letter caught the CEO, CFO, and me completely off guard. To this day we still wonder about the motivation behind the letter that darkened the dreams of a potential senior VP of marketing for a $200M company.

An effective follow-up letter should have only three objectives.

1. To show appreciation
2. To assure the company that you would like to work there
3. To ask for the job

That's it. Three short, concise paragraphs that are devoid of any statements or observations that can be misunderstood or misinterpreted.

The follow-up letter is especially valuable if you have a laid-back, passive personality. Many candidates have lost opportunities because the interviewers underestimated their interest and excitement in the company and the job. A follow-up letter may be your best avenue for removing any doubts about your level of interest.

———— ❖ ————

MISCONCEPTION

Creative, offbeat follow-up letters will hold the attention of potential employers.

REALITY

Offbeat correspondence my lead employers to think your actions are unpredictable, creating a liability for the company.

———— ❖ ————

But never try to show your interest by recommending or suggesting changes in the employer's mode of operation or management style. I recall an unusual case when Tracy, a young woman who was the leading candidate for a personnel manager's position, sent an individualized letter to each of the five people she interviewed with. Each note analyzed the strengths and needs of the recipients and their departments. Needless to say, Tracy scared the hell out of everyone and eliminated herself from the competition. Tracy's overselling was interpreted as presumptuous, negatively impacting on her chances of making the team.

An Exception to the Rule—The Need to Clarify

One situation justifies a more lengthy follow-up letter. Once the interviews are finished, if you think your discussions didn't cover all the critical areas that could get you the job, an involved letter may be in order.

To give you an illustration, Bob interviewed for three hours at dinner in a very relaxed atmosphere. This potential VP of sales appeared professional, intelligent, and well-spoken. Bob asked many probing questions about the financial condition of the company and clearly demonstrated an understanding of the accounting side of the business. However, the fact that Bob neglected to ask questions about marketing or sales strategies concerned both the CEO and me. Conversation about those key areas was so light that we considered dropping him as a candidate. Then Bob's follow-up letter arrived.

Realizing that the conversation never focused on important sales concerns, Bob carefully listed several sales and marketing issues he wished to discuss at a future date. In this case, the in-depth follow-up letter kept Bob in the running, awarded him another meeting, and eventually landed him the job.

Follow-up letters are expected by potential employers. Don't let your final representation interfere with all the hard work it took to get to the finals.

CHAPTER 17

Keeping Your Personal References in Check

At one time or another we've all heard about the world's greatest lie. You know, *The check is in the mail.* Unfortunately, most people looking for work are unaware of the four greatest myths about personal or professional references.

1. Most former employers are reluctant to talk.
2. All voluntary references provided by you result in positive feedback.
3. References are a rubber-stamp procedure used only to reinforce the decision to hire you.
4. References hardly ever eliminate you from the competition.

----------- ❖ -----------

MISCONCEPTION

Reference checks are a formality and a rubber-stamp procedure used only to verify your titles and dates of employment.

REALITY

Reference checks are fast becoming the most scrutinized area for selecting candidates.

----------- ❖ -----------

The reality in a tough market is that references can be used by potential employers to develop your work and personality profile before, not after, you make the team. Once you sign off on an employment application that authorizes contact with your references, the process could begin immediately or right after the final interviews. Therefore, it is very important to pay close attention to the reference disclosures, usually in microscopic print, at the end of every employment application.

The following discussion addresses the four most common myths about references and suggests positive steps you can take to minimize a poor reference.

Myth 1. Most Former Employers Are Reluctant to Talk

Many candidates feel that company policies prohibiting references or discussions about former employees will protect a poor work history. Wrong!

I am hard pressed to remember the last time I heard the line "It's not our policy to discuss former employees." An unwritten code bonds top executives never to intentionally hide information on a previous employee, provided the right question is asked by the interviewer.

To get to the heart of a potential candidate's character and work habits, a skilled professional will ask tough, open-ended questions that will draw an unbiased response from the former employer. I have seldom found a reference that intentionally distorted the truth. Why? RECIPROCITY. In most instances, people work within an industry for years, and someday the person giving the reference may need open feedback from the person performing the check. Make no mistake about it, managers, even competitors, talk openly about

---------------- ❖ ----------------

MISCONCEPTION

References you hand-pick always result in positive feedback.

REALITY

Many individuals with big egos will inadvertently provide negative feedback to demonstrate their level of competence.

---------------- ❖ ----------------

candidates. When managers' performances are measured by their ability to hire good people, you can be assured it's in their best interest to share information.

Myth 2. All Voluntary References Result in Positive Feedback

In a two-year period, our firm disqualified forty-one people after speaking with their references. Here are a few of the comments made by references who were hand-picked by candidates. Keep in mind that these statements came from friends, associates, and former bosses.

- "Tom is a great salesman now that he has controlled his drinking problem."
- "Sue really knocks out a lot of work; it's just too bad turnover in her department is over 50 percent. But she is working on improving relations with her people."
- "Mr. Miller is a good boss, once you learn to do it his way and only his way."
- "Judy's customers loved her, but I had to get personally involved each time we announced a price increase to ensure it stuck. Judy hated to bring bad news to her friends."
- "Bob will make a great Q.A. manager because he really cares. In fact, he's so good, he could shut your entire operation down and feel he's doing his job. Now that's a strong manager."
- "Tasha is technically astute and has great potential. I only wish we didn't have to lay her off so I could have developed Tasha into a strong contributor."

———— ❖ ————

MISCONCEPTION

References seldom eliminate you from the competition.

REALITY

Questionable references eliminate 10 to 20 percent of all candidates.

———— ❖ ————

In each of these examples, the person giving the reference truly thought he or she was helping the job seeker. Needless to say, comments like these raise the interviewer's antenna, resulting in closer scrutiny.

After years of checking hundreds of references, I have developed personality profiles on individuals most likely to inadvertently sink a candidate with an off-handed, seemingly innocent remark. My experience indicates that a person with a strong ego or one who is a little insecure has a greater tendency to talk openly during a reference check. These individuals feel compelled to compare the candidate's performance to others and demonstrate their high level of intelligence by pointing out those few little idiosyncrasies that only they would notice. GMs, sales managers, and technical directors with strong personalities and inflated egos will feel obliged to say something negative.

I remember a specific instance when our consulting firm was hiring a young account executive. Since this person was only a year out of school, we decided to forgo formal reference checks and hire this young woman on her merit. Unaware that she had been accepted for the position, her former boss, who was also a close personal friend of her family, decided to call me in an effort to push along her chances of landing the job. In thirty minutes, this friend proceeded to go into specific details concerning his strong influence on this young woman. He went on further to list short-comings she would have to conquer to meet his standards in the workplace.

---------- ❖ ----------

MISCONCEPTION

It is inappropriate to ask your references to give you feedback on their discussions with potential employers.

REALITY

It is critical that you maintain constant contact with your references to ensure the proper message is being translated to potential employers.

---------- ❖ ----------

Had I received this reference before we hired the account representative, she probably would have been eliminated as a candidate.

The bottom line? Know your *references* and ask for their honest critiques before you give their names to potential employers. Avoid getting references from people who may hurt your chances of making the team.

Myth 3. References Are a Rubber-Stamp Procedure

It wasn't long ago when unemployment was under 5 percent and technical experts in the high-tech field were as scarce as two-dollar bills.

Remember the good old days when you'd hear, "If you can put a mirror under his nose and see steam, hire 'im," or "We need more warm bodies to get these projects going"?

In fact, I recall one situation when a candidate applying for an engineering-design job actually walked out of an interview in disgust after I requested job-related references. His response was that in six interviews and five job offers, not one employer asked for references. Since people with his skills were few and far between, my client apologized to the candidate, told him references would not be necessary, and hired him on the spot. Two months later he quit. Now my client insists that final candidates submit references to be checked meticulously before any employment offer is extended.

The days of hiring without a strong background check are gone. Moreover, with the competition so keen for high-paying positions, potential employers no longer ask for voluntary references. They are requiring references from former bosses, associates, and customers.

―――――― ❖ ――――――

MISCONCEPTION

*A bad reference will automatically eliminate you
from the hunt.*

REALITY

*There is a significant difference between a bad reference
and a poor reference. Bad references confirm difficulties you
explained in the interview. Poor references come as a total
surprise to the employer and will probably result in your
elimination from the competition.*

―――――― ❖ ――――――

Our company has established guidelines requiring candidates to supply the names of all former managers over a period of ten years. If candidates cannot produce the names, they simply get cut from the competition. We refuse to sponsor candidates if we cannot speak with their former supervisors. *References are fast becoming the most important criteria in the hiring process.*

Myth 4. References Seldom Result in Elimination

Welcome to the nineties, where, as we said before, employers are going to tell you who they want as references. References will continue to be the swing factor in picking players for the team. Most companies, at reference check time, will have anywhere from two to four candidates in the running for a top position.

But before you start getting all sweaty and nervous about supplying the name of your former boss whom you called an idiot to his face, you must understand one very important distinction. There is a significant difference between a *bad reference* and a *poor reference*. A bad reference describes you in a negative light. "Jody definitely had a personality clash with the VP of marketing." A poor reference is a bad reference that comes as a complete surprise to the interviewer. "When I asked Jody, she never mentioned during the interview that she and her former boss had a poor relationship."

Bad references don't necessarily kill your chances for a job . . . poor references do.

❖

MISCONCEPTION

The majority of companies have policies that limit reference discussions to confirming dates of employment and job titles.

REALITY

There is hidden morality between employers that encourages them to communicate in an open, honest manner. If a reference you supplied won't talk, negative conclusions may be drawn.

❖

Consider the case of Paul, who was applying for a VP and general manager slot in a high-tech telecommunications company. Paul breezed through the interviews, impressed top management and the board of directors, and was ready to accept the job once his references checked out. During discussions with one reference, it was learned that Paul had recently undergone serious surgery, limiting his ability to travel. Although his medical problem was no longer a hindrance, the fact that he didn't address the subject during the interviews raised questions about his candor and honesty.

In the end, Paul was not hired as other negative factors surfaced during subsequent reference conversations. Incidentally, Paul supplied his own references, which eliminated him from the hunt, or *was it Paul who caused his own demise?*

The question now arises: Should a potential candidate prepare interviewers for the responses they might receive from references?

The answer is an emphatic *yes!* If there is any doubt in your mind that questionable matters might surface, it is right and proper to tell potential employers why you and your former boss did not agree on policies or strategies. A frank conversation with interviewers will give you an opportunity to explain the strengths and the reasoning behind your opposing viewpoints.

Potential employers don't take kindly to surprise attacks after candidates survive the cut and make it to the finals. The better you educate the potential employer to the personalities and backgrounds of the references, the less likely poor feedback will result. By

———————— ❖ ————————

MISCONCEPTION

The interviewer will tell you a poor reference knocked you out of the running.

REALITY

Potential employers, because of the fear of legal retaliation, will never reveal the source of a poor reference.

———————— ❖ ————————

alerting a potential employer to personality conflicts, you will ensure that a bad reference doesn't eliminate you from the competition.

Now for the sad revelation about poor references. You'll never be told that references knocked you out of the running. Sure, you'll hear nice words like "Your qualifications are great, but we decided to promote from within," or "After going through this process, we chose to eliminate the position," or "The other candidate just had more years of relevant experience."

What you will not hear is, "Your former boss didn't have much good to say about you," or "It's too bad that little fling you had with the CEO's secretary cost you the job."

The fear of litigation and the desire to keep lines of communication open with other industry managers will stop interviewers from revealing the source of negative statements.

So, can you ever check to confirm when you are getting a poor reference? There are two approaches that can be taken. One overt, the other covert.

The overt approach is to contact each of your references and confirm that potential employers have called. If only one of your references is contacted and the others are not, you probably have a problem with that first reference. You may then wish to ask him or her for a *Reader's Digest* version of the conversation. This way you can determine if any negatives surfaced that may have impacted on the employer's decision. All too often, employers who check references on several candidates stop and eliminate one candidate at the first sign of trouble.

---------- ❖ ----------

MISCONCEPTION

*It is immoral to set up a mock reference check when you think
negative input is being given to potential employers.*

REALITY

*If you are getting knocked out by a poor reference,
you have a right to know.*

---------- ❖ ----------

You should be aware, however, that shrewd recruiters continue checking all references even if the first one is "big league" poor. This action protects the identity of the person who may have offered the negative feedback.

If this method doesn't work out, you may wish to go underground with a bold, *covert approach*. This will alert you if you are receiving a poor reference. What you do is stage an inquiry with a friend or an associate who contacts the questionable reference.

This mock check will clearly indicate if the reference is helping or hurting your chances of making the team. If you have a strong indication that a former employer is trying to undermine you, confront the person to confirm your suspicions. Once you know the enemy, it's easy to chart a plan of attack.

If you are receiving poor references, you have a right to know. Losing out on opportunities because of a personal vendetta is totally unacceptable and should be dealt with accordingly.

It is also your responsibility to monitor the actions of your references and ensure that they are communicating with potential employers. If you know an interviewer is going to contact listed references, alert these former employers and associates to the important call. If your references don't return phone calls from potential employers, your stock will drop fast.

To be sure, the nature and mode of reference checking has changed dramatically over the years. Knowing the new rules and keeping your references in check will increase your chances of surviving the cut and making the team.

CHAPTER 18

Keeping Your Credit History on Track

Checking credit histories is not a new hiring policy. For many years, companies have performed credit checks on potential employees who would handle or have access to cash. Jobs like vending-route drivers, ticket agents and bank tellers require credit checks to identify people who might be inclined to borrow money surreptitiously.

However, in recent years, the use of a credit check as an employment tool has been expanded by most major companies to cover all professional hires. Corporations now believe credit reports tell them about your ability to handle personal finances while measuring your standard of living.

———— ❖ ————

MISCONCEPTION

Credit reports are only used when candidates are applying for positions that require handling cash.

REALITY

Credit reports are now run on most management and sales candidates.

———— ❖ ————

In addition, credit reports can predict how sales-people will treat expenses. They can also reveal insights into the likelihood of a manager staying within his or her budget and provide a quick balance sheet determining how much compensation candidates need to meet financial obligations. Too much debt usually signals short-term employees who continually search for that higher paying job.

Consider the situation of Bill, a thirty-seven-year-old regional sales manager for a major utility company who was attempting to move back into industrial sales. Bill's résumé and salary history listed earnings between $80,000 and $135,000 in three previous years. Discussions with Bill revealed that his current job provided a maximum income potential of $90,000. During our conversations, he described the expensive home he purchased in Naperville, a suburb of Chicago. He was carrying a mortgage in excess of $4,000 a month. The position he was interviewing for was a wonderful growth opportunity, but it had an earning cap of $100,000.

When Bill's credit was checked, we discovered he was two months behind on his mortgage, over his credit limit on two major credit cards, and liable for $55,000 in personal loans. Our bank's calculation estimated that Bill needed $80,000 in income just to meet his debts. Furthermore, it was estimated that he could not live comfortably on anything less than an annual income of $140,000.

———— ❖ ————

MISCONCEPTION

*Credit report information is only limited to data on
credit card balances.*

REALITY

*Credit reports provide in-depth information on payment
histories and provide a balance-sheet look at your
short- and long-term liabilities.*

———— ❖ ————

After the credit check, we understood why Bill had so many financial questions during the interview, such as, *"How soon are bonuses paid?"* and *"What dollar amount is granted as a standing advance for travel?"* Bill needed money, and he needed it fast.

History and experience dictate that people in financial trouble usually get that way because they have a tendency to spend the limit of their current income. As a group, salespeople have the most problems with poor credit because of earning fluctuations and a high-flying life-style. It is not uncommon to have salespeople fall $2,000 to $3,000 behind in expenses because they spend travel advances on personal expenditures. These overdue advances must be paid off when they leave an employer, and the money most often comes from a personal loan or an up-front signing bonus from a new employer.

In addition to making a statement about your ability to manage finances, a credit report that reveals legal suits, bankruptcies, repossessions, and foreclosures opens the door to serious questions about your character and personal habits. Individuals who have earned good salaries but have problems with finances subject themselves to questions about drug abuse, gambling, and illegal activities.

Take Sam, for example, an affable, unattached fifty-year-old looking to secure a $75,000 sales position with a high-tech component distributor. Interviews with Sam revealed that he had earned in excess of $250,000 in 1984 because of a big hit on an open-ended commission program.

——————— ❖ ———————

MISCONCEPTION

Credit reports are only read by accountants.

REALITY

Credit reports are oftentimes analyzed by a hiring manager to provide an estimate of your standard of living.

——————— ❖ ———————

The following year his employer capped his income at $150,000, resulting in a confrontation that eventually led to Sam's quitting. The most he earned in any of the following years was $85,000. Discussions with his personal references confirmed the $250,000 income and the confrontation that had followed. His story checked out.

Everything looked good until Sam's credit report came back.

Personal Bankruptcy 1987—Federal District Court

Now, think about it for a moment. He didn't have a mortgage, he earned $300,000 in one year, and two years later he filed for bankruptcy. What's your initial reaction? Well, since Sam never raised this serious issue in the interviews, and because three other qualified candidates were available for the position, Sam was quietly dropped from consideration. Later we heard through a recruiter that Sam's bankruptcy was attributed to a bad investment in a start-up company. He was on the hook for the start-up's unpaid debts. Had this information been brought up in the interview originally, Sam may have stayed in the hunt for the sales position.

A poor credit report, just like a negative reference, can eliminate you from the competition after you survived the cut.

So to determine the current state of your financial affairs, you first need to run a credit check on yourself to find out how you look on paper to an outside observer. Notations in your report such as "repossessed," "foreclosed," "bankrupt," or "charged off" will set off alarms.

---------------------- ❖ ----------------------

MISCONCEPTION

If you have had problems in the past with bad credit, it is best to keep this information to yourself.

REALITY

If you know your credit will be checked, it is advisable to discuss any problems before, not after, the employer gets the printout.

---------------------- ❖ ----------------------

Many companies specialize in securing credit reports and clearing up disputes. Your yellow pages can provide this information under the heading of "Credit Reporting Agencies."

One such company is:

TRW Credit Data
P.O. Box 749029
Dallas, TX 75374

TRW operates offices in most states. There is usually a fee for securing a personal credit report.

Your credit reports will provide another piece of valuable information—the names of individuals or companies who requested a report along with the request date. If an employer went to the expense of running a report and you never made the team, it's possible the credit report contributed to your demise.

A poor credit report can be a negative swing factor in getting a chance to play on the team. A questionable credit report may scare off a potential employer, but, like a poor reference, you'll never know it was the reason you were dropped from the competition.

So honesty is the best policy when it comes to potential problems on your credit history. If you have a credible explanation about a repossession or a foreclosure, tell the story and turn a negative event into a positive selling point.

Not raising the issue in the hope that employers will not run credit checks is like playing Russian roulette. Why take the chance? Be up-front with potential employers and control your own destiny by monitoring your own credit history.

CHAPTER 19

Travel Expenses . . . An Insight into Your Personality and Habits

The expense report you submit with your follow-up letter can foreshadow more about your habits than you would ever think.

That's right, an expense report can be a silent test of your attitude and ethics. Frequently, to travel to an interview, candidates will be asked to make their own hotel and air arrangements. What may seem like a lack of hospitality by the employer is often a test to assess your attitude toward spending company money.

The frugality you show while traveling on a potential employer's money is normally a good indicator of how you will handle their money once you come aboard.

―――――― ❖ ――――――

MISCONCEPTION

*Expense reports of candidates are never scrutinized
like those of full-time employees.*

REALITY

*Most expense reports must be signed off by the authorizing
manager and are carefully reviewed for spending habits.*

―――――― ❖ ――――――

Over the years, I have witnessed several well-qualified candidates, who excelled during the tryouts but eliminated themselves from the hunt because of the careless manner in which they handled and reported traveling expenses.

Actions that can raise an eyebrow about your character include:

- Flying first-class when coach is available
- Taking an indirect flight when a direct one is available
- Booking yourself into an expensive hotel
- Nickel and diming the expense account with entries of $1.00 or less for tolls or parking
- Spending to the limit on meal allowances
- Taking a taxi when less expensive ground transportation is available
- Making a significant number of business and personal phone calls and charging them to your room account

A case involving some of these actions led to the downfall of Pete, the perfect candidate, who had a job in his hip pocket until his expense account hit the CEO's desk for approval. This potential VP of sales and marketing for a major packaging company had a very stable work history including ten years with the same company. The question was not if, but when, Pete would be extended an offer. Then he made a few big mistakes.

———— ❖ ————

MISCONCEPTION

Flying first-class will show you have good taste and only expect the best for yourself and others.

REALITY

Flying first-class is presumptuous and the easiest way to demonstrate your lack of respect for someone else's money.

———— ❖ ————

Pete flew first-class from a Midwest city on his way to the interview in New York City with a three-hour stopover in Atlanta. This perceived act of defiance raised the CEO's blood pressure because he and his employees never flew first-class when less expensive direct flights were available. Since I was involved in the process, the CEO gave me the assignment to investigate this apparent abuse and determine if there was a reasonable explanation for Pete's expending an extra $450 to fly first-class.

When Pete was confronted with the issue, I expected a reasonable and logical justification for the expenditure. Instead Pete responded, "Other companies I've worked for only fly first-class. Plus, I needed to bump up my mileage to reach the elite fliers' club." He didn't show any remorse and was in fact somewhat insulted that I had even raised the question. He further commented that he might not want the job if that's how top executives were treated. As you can guess, Pete never had the opportunity to make the choice.

When selecting an airline, it is best to fly direct at the lowest possible fare. Booking an excursion flight demonstrates that you care about the company's money and that you can operate under less than ideal working conditions.

Also, you should always look at other expenses, such as hotels, ground transportation, meals, and miscellaneous expenditures through the eyes of the beholder, the employer.

If you are concerned that the charges for a hotel or ground transportation are too high, contact the interviewers at the company to get their suggestions on more economical alternatives. By putting the ball back into their court, you will never be accused of overspending on their nickels.

Try to keep your meal charges to a minimum and attempt to pay insignificant expenses out of your own pocket. You may also wish to avoid any charges other than the major ones for air, hotel, and ground transportation.

Instead of deducting personal phone calls from the hotel bill, charge them all on your credit card. This approach is not only more economical, but it also keeps your calls anonymous. The last thing you need is someone raising questions about your calling habits and your discretion.

And finally, if you don't get the expense check in forty-eight hours, resist the temptation to pester the company for payment. This action not only lacks professionalism but also impugns your level of trust in the potential employer.

CHAPTER 20

Accepting an Invitation to Join the Team

Once you survive the cut, shine during the tryout, and pass the scrutiny of the reference checks, the next important step in the process is to negotiate an acceptable compensation package that will provide a win-win situation for both you and your new employer.

At this stage, both you and the employer should have a pretty good handle on the parameters of your requirements. In most instances, to agree mutually on a salary and benefits, the details of the offer are informally discussed beforehand. This very delicate time in the employment process will measure your true interest in the company and the financial requirements necessary to get you on board.

———————— ❖ ————————

MISCONCEPTION

The initial offer is usually the starting point for negotiating a compensation package.

REALITY

By the time the offer is extended, most of the details regarding compensation terms should have been addressed and worked out.

———————— ❖ ————————

The negotiation should be an easy and enjoyable process. Unfortunately, two factors, or situations, can break down or halt the process.

Factor #1. Comparing Multiple Offers from Different Employers

Candidates who have solid credentials and more than one offer do have a significant negotiating advantage over individuals with only one bite. The temptation here is to get greedy, pushing the employer to the limit with your requests. But many executives will mistake these requests as demands in a bidding war for your talents.

Once it is perceived that you are using a company as a wedge to sweeten a deal, you'll most likely be dropped from further consideration. Even worse, if you are dealing with a few offers, the companies involved may get the same feeling and drop you simultaneously.

Factor #2. Focusing Too Much on Small Issues

A funny thing about negotiating . . . Most often, salaries and bonuses are not the major causes for deals falling apart. Usually, noncompensation items cause confrontations that are sometimes difficult to settle within the policy structure of the hiring company.

1. A company car
2. Insufficient relocation allowances
3. Job title
4. First-class travel
5. Payoff of advances and debts at a previous employer
6. Timing for bonus payments
7. Criteria for bonus payouts

Each of these items has the potential to become a deal breaker when it conflicts with existing company policy.

————— ❖ —————

MISCONCEPTION

It is helpful to involve friends and family members in the details of the offer.

REALITY

Monday-morning quarterbacks, because they lack all of the facts, derail more deals than you could ever imagine.

————— ❖ —————

If a company pays bonuses every six months and you desire a monthly payout, the exception to the policy may be too difficult to overcome. Therefore, you should look at the total picture and determine if you really want to work for the employer before exceptions are granted. If you push the employer to the wall, win your point, then end up refusing the offer, you could do substantial damage to your reputation.

You should be aware that potential employers also keep a watchful eye on the outside influences that affect your decisions. Street-smart executives know when your demands are being shaped by your spouse or friends. For example, if you never raised an issue about extra vacation time during the interviews and only bring it up after reviewing the compensation terms with your spouse, the employer will be concerned with your ability to withstand pressure when you have to make a tough decision.

Take the case of Mark, who sailed through the interview process and was extended a wonderful offer that topped his former salary by 20 percent. He accepted the offer with the final comment, "I can't wait to tell my wife."

The following day, the personnel director who extended the offer received an unusual call. Mark started asking about termination clauses, extra vacation time, stock options, and a few other perks that had never been raised during any previous discussions. Out of curiosity, the personnel director asked Mark why he hadn't raised these issues before the formal letter of offer had been drafted. He candidly stated that his wife was an ex-personnel manager who thought the offer lacked too many specifics. Mark was then instructed to prepare a list of his requirements and fax them the next day.

That night, Mark and his wife apparently conjured up eleven different items, which had nothing to do with direct compensation. Two days after he submitted his demands, Mark received a letter. The company withdrew the offer because of the additional conditions of employment.

So be careful with Monday-morning quarterbacks who think they know what is best for you.

If you are going to negotiate . . . *request* . . . *don't demand*. Keep your sights focused on the major issues like salary and incentive compensation. Too much nit-picking will provide an employer with ammunition to shoot you down from consideration. Remember, a job in the hand is better than three potential offers in the mail.

About The Author

Kevin J. Murphy is a well-known international author, consultant, and speaker on effective communications.

Mr. Murphy is the author of several books, including *Thanks for the Order–Selling Through Listening, Effective Listening–Your Key to Career Success, What Did He Say?–Management Through Listening,* and *Management That Works–Common-Sense Approaches That Build A Proud, Responsive Company.*

Mr. Murphy addresses businesses and trade groups on the use of listening skills to interview, select, and motivate employees. Frequently quoted in major publications such as *Fortune, Reader's Digest,* and *USA Today,* Mr. Murphy has appeared on national television programs such as CNN and Lifetime.

He is president of CDK Associates & Consultants, Inc., a consulting firm that specializes in personnel evaluations, customer and employee opinion surveys, and outplacement counseling.

Mr. Murphy is also the founder of the Effective Listening® Institute, a training firm that conducts writing and listening programs for trade groups and businesses.

His current clients include companies in such diverse markets as health care, building products, chemicals, plastics, telecommunications, textiles, packaging, and automotive.

CDK Associates & Consultants, Inc. has offices in Salem, New Hampshire and Orlando, Florida.